BASICS

FASHION DE

04

Elinor Renfrew
Colin Renfrew

DEVELOPING
A COLLECTION

Ethical: aware-
ness/
reflect-
ion/
debate

ava
academia

An AVA Book
Published by AVA Publishing SA
Rue des Fontenailles 16
Case Postale
1000 Lausanne 6
Switzerland
Tel: +41 786 005 109
Email: enquiries@avabooks.ch

Distributed by Thames & Hudson (ex-North America)
181a High Holborn
London WC1V 7QX
United Kingdom
Tel: +44 20 7845 5000
Fax: +44 20 7845 5055
Email: sales@thameshudson.co.uk
www.thamesandhudson.com

Distributed in the USA & Canada by:
Ingram Publisher Services Inc.
1 Ingram Blvd.
La Vergne TN 37086
USA
Tel: +1 866 400 5351
Fax: +1 800 838 1149
Email: customer.service@ingrampublisherservices.com

English Language Support Office
AVA Publishing (UK) Ltd.
Tel: +44 1903 204 455
Email: enquiries@avabooks.ch

ISBN 978-2-940373-95-6
10 9 8 7 6 5 4 3 2 1

Design by Sifer Design
Cover illustration courtesy of Giles Deacon

Production by AVA Book Production Pte. Ltd., Singapore
Tel: +65 6334 8173
Fax: +65 6259 9830
Email: production@avabooks.com.sg

All reasonable attempts have been made to trace, clear and credit the
copyright holders of the images reproduced in this book. However, if any
credits have been inadvertently omitted, the publisher will endeavour to
incorporate amendments in future editions.

1

Contents

1   Backstage at Prada A/W08.
     Catwalking.com.

'I also like to work on fabrics that supposedly don't sell, like kid mohair. I was forbidden to use it but of course it became a best-seller for us.'

Miuccia Prada

All designers go through the same stages when developing a collection. Whether they have their own label or are employed by a large company, the starting point and processes are invariably the same: research, design, development, editing and presentation.

Basics Fashion Design: Developing a Collection will guide you through the different aspects of the development process. The first chapter asks 'What is a collection?' It provides an overview, explaining who and what is involved. Chapter 2 looks at the common themes used by designers, from global and political influences to the more abstract themes of humour and fantasy. Chapters 3 and 4 introduce different types of collections: looking at market level, from haute couture to the high street; and specialist collections, such as children's wear and jewellery. The final chapter is focused on you, as a student, to give you guidelines and inspiration for designing your own degree collection.

Underpinning each chapter are interviews with designers from all over the fashion industry, who share their own experiences of developing collections. These exclusive interviews include illustrations and archive images.

Basics Fashion Design: Developing a Collection is richly illustrated with images from international collections, both on and off the catwalk, in addition to archive material.

How to get the most out of this book

This book introduces different aspects of developing a collection. Each chapter provides numerous examples of collections by leading designers, annotated to explain the reasons behind the choices made.

Key fashion design and development principles are isolated so that the reader can see how they are applied in practice.

Captions
These provide image details and commentary to guide the reader in the exploration of the visuals displayed.

Examples
Imagery accompanying the content, visually describing design development and inspirational collections.

The team

1   Yves Saint Laurent in his design studio in Paris, 1965.

2   Gilles Deacon backstage at his A/W08 show. Catwalking.com.

The development process is cyclical and dependent upon a number of team members and specialist activities. The team will usually consist of a designer, a pattern cutter, sample cutter, sample machinist and a costing/production manager. There may also be people who specialise in sourcing fabric and trims, print designers and graphic designers.

As the number of collections being developed increases, so too will the number of staff in the team or business. Many larger companies (designer and retail) have established separate business units or divisions to cater for the business demands and development processes involved. As such, within the largest fashion businesses, it is possible to have senior design positions with a responsibility for a very specific product area, such as men's casual knitwear or women's jersey separates.

The designer

The designer is the central member of the team and he or she is ultimately responsible for creating the collection, from the initial design stages, right through to overseeing first samples for selling. The designer will brief a team of assistants or the studio staff to create further research or feedback for development.

Designers can have multiple working relations, dealing with everyone from fabric and trim merchants, yarn suppliers and textile designers to buyers, merchandisers, costing clerks, accountants and PR agents. The designer will take the responsibility for all decision making and amendments to any aspect of the process. The ability to communicate is just as important as being creative; in fact, it is often key to success.

Introductions
Special section introductions outline basic concepts that will be discussed.

Developing a Collection

Clear navigation
Each chapter has a clear heading to allow readers to quickly locate areas of interest.

Headings
These enable the reader to break down text and refer quickly to topics of interest.

Additional information
Box-outs elaborate on subjects discussed in the main text.

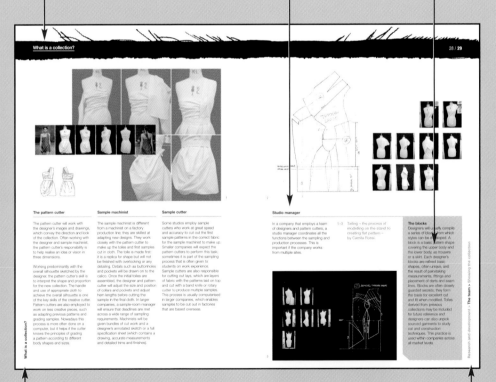

The pattern cutter

The pattern cutter will work with the designer's images and drawings, which convey the direction and look of the collection. Often working with the designer and sample machinist, the pattern cutter's responsibility is to help realise an idea or vision in three dimensions.

Working predominantly with the overall silhouette sketched by the designer, the pattern cutter's skill is to interpret the shape and proportion for the new collection. The handle and use of appropriate cloth to achieve the overall silhouette is one of the key skills of the creative cutter. Pattern cutters are also employed to work on less creative pieces, such as adapting previous patterns and grading samples. Nowadays this process is more often done on a computer, but it helps if the cutter knows the principles of grading a pattern according to different body shapes and sizes.

Sample machinist

The sample machinist is different from a machinist on a factory production line; they are skilled at adapting new designs. They work closely with the pattern cutter to make up the toiles and first samples cut in cloth. The toile is made first; it is a replica for shape but will not be finished with overlocking or any detailing. Details such as buttonholes and pockets will be drawn on to the calico. Once the initial toiles are assembled, the designer and pattern cutter will adjust the size and position of collars and pockets and adjust hem lengths before cutting the sample in the final cloth. In larger companies, a sample-room manager will ensure that deadlines are met across a wide range of sampling requirements. Machinists will be given bundles of cut work and a designer's annotated sketch or a full specification sheet (which contains a drawing, accurate measurements and detailed trims and finishes).

Sample cutter

Some studios employ sample cutters who work at great speed and accuracy to cut out the first sample patterns in the correct fabric for the sample machinist to make up. Smaller companies will expect the pattern cutters to perform this task, sometimes it is part of the sampling process that is often given to students on work experience. Sample cutters are also responsible for cutting out lays, which are layers of fabric with the patterns laid on top and cut with a band knife or rotary cutter to produce multiple samples. This process is usually computerised in larger companies, which enables samples to be cut out in factories that are based overseas.

Studio manager

In a company that employs a team of designers and pattern cutters, a studio manager coordinates all the functions between the sampling and production processes. This is important if the company works from multiple sites.

1–0   Toiling – the process of modelling on the stand to creating flat pattern – by Camilla Rossi.

The blocks

Designers will usually compile a series of blocks from which styles can be developed. A block is a basic pattern shape covering the upper body and the lower body, as trousers or a skirt. Each designer's blocks are refined basic shapes, often unique, and the result of painstaking measurements, fittings and placement of darts and seam lines. Blocks are often closely guarded secrets; they form the basis for excellent cut and fit when modified. Toiles derived from previous collections may be included for future reference and designers can also unpick sourced garments to study cut and construction techniques. This practice is used within companies across all market levels.

What is a collection?

Research and development > **The team** > Showing the collection

Chapter titles
These run along the bottom of every page to provide clear navigation and allow the reader to understand the context of the information on the page.

Running footers
Clear navigation allows the reader to know where they are, where they have come from and where they are going in the book.

How to get the most out of this book

'All creation is just recreation – a new way of seeing the same things and expressing them differently.'

Yves Saint Laurent

A collection is a range of garments, accessories or products that are designed and produced for sale to retailers or direct to customers. This range of pieces may be inspired by a trend, theme or design direction reflecting cultural and social influences, and it is usually designed for a season or particular occasion. A collection is a grouping of outfits or looks that are presented in a variety of ways, from catwalk presentations to online web pages. Collections are usually constructed from a combination of silhouettes, colours and fabrics, with the emphasis varying depending on the designer's particular aesthetic. This chapter introduces the concept of the collection. It explains who and what is involved in the development process, from the early design stages through to production and promotion.

1

How to start a collection

Any successful or financially viable collection requires an enormous amount of research, investigation and planning. Successful designers, manufacturers and retailers have a clear understanding of their customers' needs as well as understanding their position in a highly competitive market. In addition to the creation and realisation of any collection, there are a range of issues that need to be considered if the final garments are to hang in customers' wardrobes. For example, a collection may include a range of white shirts. If the cut, construction and retail price is favourable and there is a customer base for the shirts, and if the range is delivered to stores at the right time and the stores pay for the stock within an agreed time frame, then there is a good chance that this is enough to start a fashion business. By offering a product that is not currently available, or one with an added-value quality, fashion buyers will consider stocking pieces from the collection. If the pieces sell quickly (and therefore at full retail price) there is an opportunity for the buyer to either reorder and replace stock or plan to order the following season.

1   Christian Dior menswear
     S/S08. Belgian designer Kris
     Van Assche's debut
     collection for Dior Homme,
     showing a tableau of male
     models in white evening
     shirts with 1980s-inspired
     trousers. The arrangement
     reflects Irving Penn's classic
     group of couture models.
     Catwalking.com.

How to start a collection > Research and development

1

Market research

In order to gain an understanding of current fashion stock and ranges across market levels, many, if not all, designers will conduct a 'comp shop'. This term refers to comparing stock in competitor retail outlets, regardless of market level. Quality of fabric, construction and detailing are carefully studied alongside prices and origin of manufacture. This provides a great deal of information that is useful when planning and selling a fashion collection. Ultimately, it will be the fashion buyers who make the decision to order fashion ranges and their decisions are based on a combination of the following: historical knowledge of their particular customers; sales figures, which track how many items of each piece within a collection were bought the previous season; delivery and availability of stock; quality of merchandise; exclusivity; and price. Designers are increasingly producing pre-collections in addition to the main seasonal collections. For example Stefano Pilati, design

director at YSL, designs up to 20 collections a year, covering every occasion for menswear and womenswear. The pre-collection will account for up to 80 per cent of the season's sales, with main catwalk collections aimed at press and publicity.

Many small fashion businesses lack the infrastructure to provide accurate market and marketing information. However, intuition and awareness of fashion directions will help a start-up label become commercially successful. The buyers are usually cautious when adopting new designers and therefore use a system of sale or return, which offers new talent the opportunity to showcase their collections alongside more established brands; they can then be picked up as the next new name if their collections sells. Another way of launching a new fashion business is by concentrating on one particular piece. Many successful designers have started

this way, later expanding into a range of product areas based on their hero product. For example, Calvin Klein's first collection was a range of women's coats and Ralph Lauren began his vast empire with a small collection of ties.

Buying and selling presents a challenge in predicting how much fabric will be required for production of orders, and the possibility of reordering within a season. Too much fabric can result in funds tied up in stock, which then needs to be sold or reused. Too little fabric ordered can result in lost sales and reduced profits. The same consideration must be given to production time – whether it is a small team of machinists or a large-scale factory.

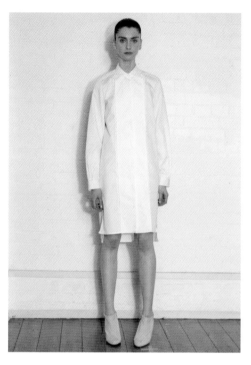

1   A look book showing a
    white shirt collection by
    Richard Nicoll.

Identifying the customer

The muse

Ideal or inspirational customers are sometimes known as a 'muse' – usually a woman – who embodies the designer's style or approach to fashion. Many designers will adopt a muse who will act as a supplementary input into the development of each collection. John Galliano worked with Lady Amanda Harlech, only to lose her to Karl Lagerfeld at Chanel, where her input continues as part of the design process. Models may also be influential figures – either through their own personal style, or as a 'face' to be used in advertising campaigns for the designer or the brand.

By careful investigation and competitor analysis, designers can begin to identify a specific market area and customer for their fashion vision. At times, designers will create an imaginary situation where characters are involved in a plot, journey or scenario. Characters may be well-known historical figures or completely fictitious, but this collage of people and events can provide a rich starting point for imagining, visualising and defining colours, fabrics and shapes without constraints. John Galliano's collections exemplify this method and his designs illustrate the huge range of possibilities in collaging fragments of inspiration. Whilst this makes for a romantic or stylised approach to customer profiling, most large companies are able to define every aspect of their customers through sales and specialist marketing information.

This information takes into account social and economic influences and how customers' lives are defined by a range of factors. Successful fashion producers are able to define their customers in relation to the business, from the past and present to the future. It is possible to start with a fashion view, or purist approach to fashion, where an aspect of the process – perhaps creative cutting – informs the final pieces. The customer, occasion and cost remain considerations if the final garments are to work in any commercial context. However, not all pieces within a collection are designed on a commercial basis. Catwalk showpieces work as a promotional tool to attract the press, which helps to reinforce the designer's popularity and currency.

1   Stephen Jones has collaborated with John Galliano for over 15 years. John Galliano S/S09. Catwalking.com.

2   Illustration by Stephen Jones.

Creativity versus wearability

'What really makes Stephen's millinery so unique is his personality, his elegance and refinement. Everything he does looks simply blown together. That is the art of millinery.'

John Galliano

Creativity is a subjective issue, as all fashion expresses a creative vision and process. Wearability is also subjective and rests with the consumer, who can make personal judgements about self-image, acceptability and suitability, depending on occasion or lifestyle. Today's consumer is inundated with fashion choices and the media's infatuation with fashion, celebrity and influence provides enormous coverage of how fashion and style can be portrayed. Many designers will create extravagant showpieces – whether they are hats, shoes or garments – which are deliberately included to excite the fashion press and gain maximum

coverage. Established fashion houses stage catwalk shows for both haute couture and prêt-à-porter and designers are encouraged to create spectacular, theatrical shows as a prelude to the advertising campaigns. Showpieces are often the result of creative collaboration. John Galliano, for example, collaborates with milliner Stephen Jones and Alexander McQueen collaborates with milliner Philip Treacy to enhance their catwalk statements. This type of collection is more about storytelling than sales. Other designers are innovative in the way they present their collections at low cost, by staging shows in

unusual venues and presenting the clothes in experimental new ways. But irrespective of the approach, whatever the market level and customer, the commercial reality is that creativity and wearability are mutually interdependent if a fashion business is to succeed.

2

Research and development

Themes and directions for collections can be enhanced and developed from primary research, regardless of location, time or season. The research process is an ongoing aspect of the designer's role and it is unlikely to start from scratch.

When developing a collection with the staff team on-site, the designer will begin by explaining the overall look or theme for the new collection. This may be in the form of images and drawings on inspiration or mood boards, as well as sourced garments, fabric cuttings (sometimes taken from vintage garments) and trims, all of which may be key to the new collection. After discussing shapes and fabrics, the first patterns and toiles will be prepared. These toiles will be recut and refined a number of times in the process from initial idea to final reality. Most designers and manufacturers will hire a model, known as a fit or house model. This is crucial in refining and confirming exact proportions, detail placement, movement and overall look. Models are hired specifically for their height and body

1

1   Designer > inspiration > visualisation > briefing to sample team, including pattern cutter, sample maker and finance (costing and business).

5   Designer > show producer for venue, music, set, ticketing, models, hair and make-up.

2   Designer > business manager for final costings and ordering for production (materials and manufacturing time).

4   Designer > business manager and retail buyers to establish orders and confirm production.

3   Designer > stylist for final show presentation.

dimensions, as this information will be crucial to the pattern cutter and also when casting models for a show. Once garments have been bought for retail they will be resized, with changes made to length, proportion and so on. This is important if exporting to some international markets, or may simply reflect the type of customer, who may demand a less extreme version of the showpieces.

Depending on the season being developed, additional specialist freelance team members may be contracted to work to specific pieces or looks. These may include knitwear specialists, beading specialists, embroiderers, hand-craft tailors or fashion-print designers. As the team grows and the variables within a collection increase, the designer must control this range of activities to ensure that the original vision or brief is still in view. Freelance designers who contribute to the collection may be briefed at the onset or commissioned to produce individual pieces, such as shoes or hats, which will highlight a particular aspect of the collection.

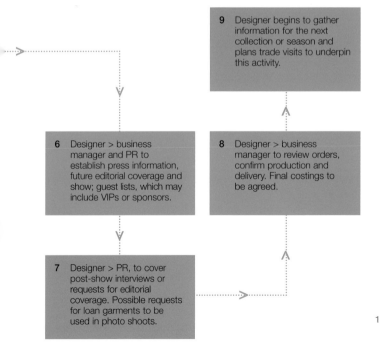

9   Designer begins to gather information for the next collection or season and plans trade visits to underpin this activity.

6   Designer > business manager and PR to establish press information, future editorial coverage and show; guest lists, which may include VIPs or sponsors.

8   Designer > business manager to review orders, confirm production and delivery. Final costings to be agreed.

7   Designer > PR, to cover post-show interviews or requests for editorial coverage. Possible requests for loan garments to be used in photo shoots.

1   This diagram illustrates each stage in the process of developing a collection.

Fabric fairs

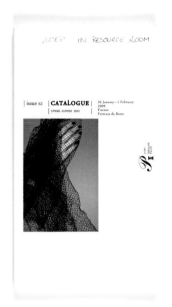

1

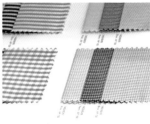

2

A key part of the designer's role is sourcing fabric and they will visit trade fairs twice a year before the start of the following season to source the newest fabrics (or, if they have an established relationship with fabric mills, they may develop their own fabrics). Première Vision is the most famous of the fashion fabric and trend exhibitions and draws designers and manufacturers from across the world. Other fairs include Pitti Filati in Florence, which deals mainly with yarns and colour, and Linea Pelle in Bologna, which specifically deals with leather and leather-based products and trends. Première Vision, Pitti Filati and

Linea Pelle are staged twice a year, usually in January or February and June or July. Another fabric fair, Texworld, covers fabric produced in the Far East at a sixth of the cost of European fabrics and is becoming more and more popular because it offers a cheaper alternative to Première Vision. Smaller fairs are also emerging, such as Tissu Lille in France and the Turkish Fabric Fair in London, which welcomes students, as well as designers. Trend direction information is gathered from the vast range of exhibitors.

At all the fairs manufacturers display their ranges on fabric hangers, often organised as trends or stories. Designers and manufacturers visit these exhibitions with a view to order sample lengths, which are delivered in time to plan and develop the new season's ranges. Most exhibitors at Première Vision are happy to deal with business of all sizes for sample orders, but have a required minimum order to ensure production is viable for particular prints, colourways or fabrics. For smaller orders, manufacturers may levy a surcharge or combine the orders, which delays delivery time. A number of the more established designers will request certain fabrics, prints or colourways as an exclusive purchase. This additional cost is passed on to the customer and is reflected in the final garment's price.

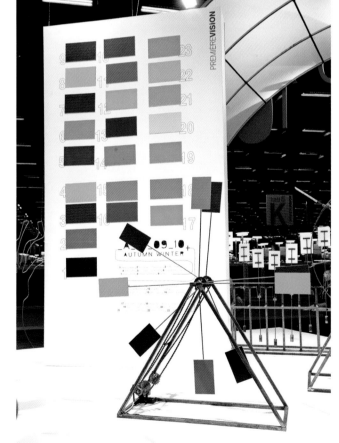

1   A selection of trade fair catalogues: Première Vision and Tissu Premier are the main fabric shows and Pitti Filati showcases yarns.

2   A sample book of shirtings by Ringhart.

3–4 Trade stands at fabric fair Première Vision.

How to start a collection > **Research and development** > The team

Trend forecasting

Existing and emerging fashion trends constantly provide stimulus and trend information is seen as a key element across all the creative industries. Traditionally, trends have been identified and packaged for designers as forecasting packages, where colours, fabrics, yarns, silhouettes and graphics are collated into books or presented online and used to predict key looks for the forthcoming season. This detailed trend information may inform or influence a collection in greater depth than a single season's direction or look.

Trend forecasting companies or futurologists will give presentations internally to larger organisations to establish a direction based on the client's needs and aspirations. One example is Li Edelkoort's Paris-based forecasting company, Trend Union, which produces the magazines *View on Colour* and *Bloom*. Clients use these prediction manuals as starting points for their next collections. Li Edelkoort's aim is to 'open the imagination of our clients and act as a stimulus. The books give a new direction, but it's up to the client to interpret and take further.'

As fashion has evolved and information sources are now widely available online, the trend forecasting industry has responded to provide a wider range of products. These include trend intelligence, trend management, international retail trends, customer trends, advertising, catwalk shows and technology trends; all available by subscription. Another forecasting agency, Studio M, based in London, works closely with clients all over the world to produce bespoke packages for inspiration. They take influences from tear sheets, photographs, objects, fabric taken from source

pieces, paintings or any other imagery that complements the story, and use them to create A1 trend boards. They can dip-dye a series of colour swatches on base fabrics to create a palette; provide samples of embroidery and specialist trims; and remake elements such as collars taken from vintage garments to interpret looks. By offering a full service, clients can then pick and choose elements as required for their own collections.

1   A montage of trend boards by Studio M.

2   Trend information by Studio M, incorporating fashion flats.

Trend companies
www.thefuturelaboratory.com
www.carlininternational.com
www.trendstop.com
www.fashioninformation.com
www.promostyl.com
www.kjaer-global.com
www.stylesignal.com

1

2

Archiving

Archiving is now common across all levels of the fashion market, where discarded ideas or prototypes can be revisited and reconsidered for future collections. Source pieces can include items from a designer's own archive of past collections. These pieces may form part of a new collection, as replicas cut in different fabrics or prints, for example, or may instead influence fresh development. Sometimes a collection can be created using 'rails' or 'grids' where images, garments and fabrics are collated into a three-dimensional collage that captures a theme or design direction, illustrating the colour, shapes and details involved to create a cohesive look. This is useful for all team members involved in the development and realisation processes and it helps to inform decision making. It is important to note that the processes involved are evolutionary and changes, additions and deletions will occur throughout the development time frame. Research and development activities are interactive and often dictate even last-minute revisions and changes. The designer or design director will have the overall and final decision on the complete collection content and look.

Photographic archiving is used to record the development of draped toiles on stands as staged versions of an idea, or images of the collection in individual outfits or looks. The latter is useful when allocating outfits to individual models and planning the running order for a fashion show. Many designers use photography to compile images for possible research and, because much of the collection's development is visually based, this saves time and establishes a common visual language. Photography plays an enormous part in the documentation, development and archiving of fashion garments. With the accessibility of digital photography and wireless technology, it is now possible for designers to source and collate an endless number of images for personal reference databases.

Editing collections

Regardless of how or when a designer begins a new collection, there will inevitably be problems that challenge the most careful planning. Deliveries, mistakes and delays are variables that must be expected and managed. Additional problems can occur when the designer subcontracts or employs freelance specialists to collaborate on the collection and the final show.

Even when most pieces are complete, fitted and photographed as outfits or looks, further changes may be required if the whole collection is adrift of the original vision, or the range is imbalanced in colour, garment type or fabric. During the development cycle, it is very common for ideas to be rejected, for new aspects to be introduced to the collection plan, and for nearly everything to run late. Whilst this is the popular view of the

creative process involved within the fashion industry, it accurately acknowledges the complexity and convergent energies involved.

Editorial decisions are based on the whole collection working as envisaged at the outset. The designer may acknowledge that some pieces or outfits have not worked as well as hoped, or may perhaps look repetitive. Changes or rejections exist as part of the development process and are common at every market level.

Useful archive sources
Wayne Hemingway set up an online archive for the Land of Lost Content museum. This huge collection of popular British culture images is a useful resource for students and industry alike.
<www.lolc.org.uk>

1   A series of boards by Holly Berry, showing photographic archiving.

2   Final, edited collection by Kingston graduate Alison Gaukroger.

2

The team

1   Yves Saint Laurent in his
    design studio in Paris, 1965.

2   Giles Deacon backstage
    at his A/W09 show.
    Catwalking.com.

The development process is cyclical and dependent upon a number of team members and specialist activities. The team will usually consist of a designer, a pattern cutter, sample cutter, sample machinist and a costing/production manager. There may also be people who specialise in sourcing fabric and trims, print designers and graphic designers.

As the number of collections being developed increases, so too will the number of staff in the team or business. Many larger companies (designer and retail) have established separate business units or divisions to cater for the business demands and development processes involved. As such, within the largest fashion businesses, it is possible to have senior design positions with a responsibility for a very specific product area, such as men's casual knitwear or women's jersey separates.

1

The designer

The designer is the central member of the team and he or she is ultimately responsible for creating the collection, from the initial design stages, right through to overseeing first samples for selling. The designer will brief a team of assistants or the studio staff to create further research or feedback for development.

Designers can have multiple working relations, dealing with everyone from fabric and trim merchants, yarn suppliers and textile designers to buyers, merchandisers, costing clerks, accountants and PR agents. The designer will take the responsibility for all decision making and amendments to any aspect of the process. The ability to communicate is just as important as being creative; in fact, it is often key to success.

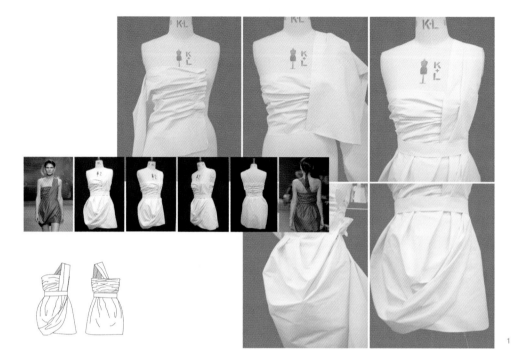

1

The pattern cutter

The pattern cutter will work with the designer's images and drawings, which convey the direction and look of the collection. Often working with the designer and sample machinist, the pattern cutter's responsibility is to help realise an idea or vision in three dimensions.

Working predominantly with the overall silhouette sketched by the designer, the pattern cutter's skill is to interpret the shape and proportion for the new collection. The handle and use of appropriate cloth to achieve the overall silhouette is one of the key skills of the creative cutter. Pattern cutters are also employed to work on less creative pieces, such as adapting previous patterns and grading samples. Nowadays this process is more often done on a computer, but it helps if the cutter knows the principles of grading a pattern according to different body shapes and sizes.

Sample machinist

The sample machinist is different from a machinist on a factory production line; they are skilled at adapting new designs. They work closely with the pattern cutter to make up the toiles and first samples cut in cloth. The toile is made first: it is a replica for shape but will not be finished with overlocking or any detailing. Details such as buttonholes and pockets will be drawn on to the calico. Once the initial toiles are assembled, the designer and pattern cutter will adjust the size and position of collars and pockets and adjust hem lengths before cutting the sample in the final cloth. In larger companies, a sample-room manager will ensure that deadlines are met across a wide range of sampling requirements. Machinists will be given bundles of cut work and a designer's annotated sketch or a full specification sheet (which contains a drawing, accurate measurements and detailed trims and finishes).

Sample cutter

Some studios employ sample cutters who work at great speed and accuracy to cut out the first sample patterns in the correct fabric for the sample machinist to make up. Smaller companies will expect the pattern cutters to perform this task; sometimes it is part of the sampling process that is often given to students on work experience. Sample cutters are also responsible for cutting out lays, which are layers of fabric with the patterns laid on top and cut with a band knife or rotary cutter to produce multiple samples. This process is usually computerised in larger companies, which enables samples to be cut out in factories that are based overseas.

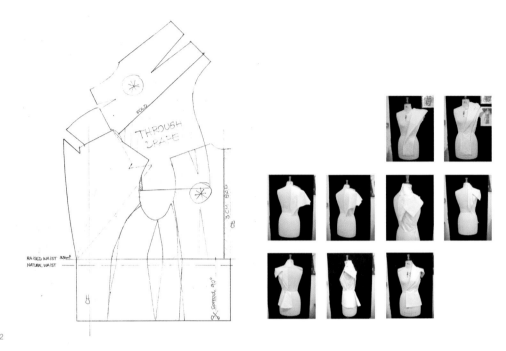

2

Studio manager

In a company that employs a team of designers and pattern cutters, a studio manager coordinates all the functions between the sampling and production processes. This is important if the company works from multiple sites.

1–3 Toiling – the process of modelling on the stand to creating flat pattern – by Camila Rossi.

The blocks

Designers will usually compile a series of blocks from which styles can be developed. A block is a basic pattern shape covering the upper body and the lower body, as trousers or a skirt. Each designer's blocks are refined basic shapes, often unique, and the result of painstaking measurements, fittings and placement of darts and seam lines. Blocks are often closely guarded secrets; they form the basis for excellent cut and fit when modified. Toiles derived from previous collections may be included for future reference and designers can also unpick sourced garments to study cut and construction techniques. This practice is used within companies across all market levels.

3

Costing manager

All garments within a collection that are produced to sell must be costed. This is either the responsibility of the designer or, in larger companies, a costing administrator. Costings are based on two main components: materials (direct cost) and labour (indirect cost). Costings are a key part of technical packs, which include detailed specification sheets of sketches, measurements, fabric and trim references and special instructions for finishes.

The costing process links sampling and production and ensures that the designer's vision is carried through to the shop floor. Samples are reworked and sometimes fabrics substituted if the cost is too high after margins are added (margins can be up to 250 per cent for some stores to cover their costs). Samples are being increasingly sent to factories in the Far East to be copied at a far cheaper rate for both fabric and labour. But with the current and increasing emphasis on sustainable and organic fabrics, costs are also increasing so marketing plays an important part in promoting the added value and social conscience.

Buyers and merchandisers

Fashion buyers are judged by sales and departmental profitability. As such, most buyers are keen to investigate new lines or designers capable of adding to an established retail business. Quality, reliability of delivery and reordering are essential considerations in addition to cost. The relationship between designers and buyers is important and can launch a successful career, such as Joan Burstein at Browns in London, who bought John Galliano's graduation collection and featured it in the store's windows.

In large, multiple companies the role of the merchandiser is equal to that of the designer; they often work together to create and edit the collection to a price. Merchandisers are responsible for the pieces of a collection that end up in store. They are accountants and decision makers with a creative understanding for the product. In the USA the merchandiser is the designer's other half. In the UK, however, merchandisers deal with figures and quantities, working alongside the buyers, who are responsible for ranging and selecting from the directive of the design team. Working to budgets, the designer, merchandiser and buyer are all responsible for a company's commercial success.

Stylists and PR agents

Designers and producers will work with a fashion stylist when considering the presentation of the collection for press, buyers or the consumer. Usually working on a freelance basis, the stylist will oversee each element of the collection to ensure that the original vision is realised. The stylist may also be the main contact person for coordinating a catwalk show; they can work on footwear, accessories, hair and make-up, as well as the music used as part of the show. Experienced stylists transform the most basic fashion piece into a key look or trend and inspire a wider audience of designers and producers.

PR agents can also work in a stylist capacity, being responsible for the look of the catwalk show and working with photographers to create editorial and advertising for magazines. PR agents also distribute look books and arrange appointments with buyers.

1   Designer Natsumi Zama
     fitting a final garment for
     a photo shoot.

Resources

A typical start-up designer business may well be located in small or adapted premises. The basic requirements, if samples are to be made in the design studio, are a cutting table, industrial machines and pressing equipment. There should be allocated space for storage of fabrics (current season sampling fabric and production fabric), trims, pattern paper, final patterns and hanging equipment. A space for meetings and showroom for visitors is desirable for a professional appearance. Most rental spaces for fashion companies will be configured to allow for all these functions. Depending on how a collection is produced, it is common to outsource most activities to specialist providers such as pattern cutters and sample makers. This relies on subcontractors or 'cut, make and trim' outworker units being able to understand the designer's requirements and specifications.

Regardless of the exact provision of resources, overheads and costs must be carefully managed and built into the garment costings. Many designers starting out with a new fashion label fail due to inadequate knowledge of the business side. Some of the most successful designers, such as Yves Saint Laurent, Giorgio Armani and UK designer Betty Jackson founded their businesses with a business or financial expert – thereby allowing clear role definitions within the company.

1

Showing the collection

1   Look book of graduate
collection by Nicolas Barton.

2   Shelley Fox's Philadelphia
Florist exhibition at the
Stanley Picker Gallery,
Kingston University.

Most designer collections are shown internationally as part of a
seasonal show schedule of spring/summer and autumn/winter.
This traditional method of showing the latest looks is the same in
every fashion capital, with a week-long schedule of fashion shows
attracting buyers and press. Major fashion houses rely on these
shows to promote their brand and will more often sell through a
smaller salon show or exhibition to targeted clients or through
pre-collections aimed specifically at loyal customers. But increasingly
designers are choosing to show their work in alternative ways, either
through an exhibition, installation or online presentation. Nick Knight's
broadcasting website <www.showstudio.com> showcased Shelley
Fox's early installations. The website continues to promote alternative
ways of showing collections. He promotes the work of Gareth Pugh
and Aitor Thorp, showing films of their installations instead of
traditional catwalk shows. Some designers' collections are based
on fashion as fine-art pieces or collaborations with artists. These
garments may be influential to fashion designers but are rarely seen
as fashion pieces: they are not intended to be worn as clothing, but
serve to broaden our perceptions of clothes.

For example, in the 1930s, Elsa Schiaparelli collaborated with surrealist artist Salvador Dali to create playful trompe l'oeil prints and accessories. This collaboration was intellectually interesting, highly influential and is still referenced today. Fashion designer and artist Lucy Orta <www.studio-orta.com> uses garments as a narrative element within a series of internationally acclaimed exhibitions. There is no immediate fashion application to these images, yet the influence of this work can inform the fashion process and consumer.

Another example of fashion collections showcased for enjoyment, rather than immediate commercial application, is the curated exhibition, such as 'Superheroes: Fashion and Fantasy' at the Metropolitan Museum of Art in New York, a thematically curated exhibition of fashion pieces based on comic-book characters and their style. In addition, retrospective exhibitions, designed to celebrate a designer's career, may create a fresh interest in a particular style or look. Examples include Giorgio Armani, Viktor & Rolf and Bill Gibb.

Capsule collections
Some designers offer an additional, smaller collection in December/January, known as the cruise collection (or holiday collection in the USA). These collections are primarily summer lines, prepared and available before the new spring ranges are fully delivered into stores. Cruise collections are popular with wealthy customers who holiday at this time of year. Increasingly clients want exclusivity. Designers such as Nicolas Ghesquière at Balenciaga have reintroduced specialist capsule collections. Similar to haute couture, these collections are shown to private customers and are not available to a wider audience.

2

1

Look books

Whilst often spectacular, fashion shows may not be necessary for commercial success. Although the catwalk shows are attended by buyers and press, the pieces bought for retail may be significantly different (i.e. more wearable) and are selected before the season's collection is shown. Designers and retailers compile each collection into a look book, where each piece is ranged as looks and photographed as such. Away from the catwalk, decisions are made on what the customer will want when the items are available. This buying or selection process may take place on the designer's premises or else in a rented studio. Designers who show in London, for example, may be invited to sell at events such as Trenois or Rendez-Vous in Paris. They can rent a salon for the duration of the selling period – usually up to two weeks – so that buyers can make appointments to see the collection.

1   Menswear look book by Chris Owen.

2   Look book of A/W09 collection by Danielle Scutt.

The team > **Showing the collection** > Giles Deacon

1

Catwalk shows

Catwalk presentations are a way of showing collections in an experiential, idealised context in order to create press coverage as well as orders. Costs and workload increase dramatically and at times may create no orders for the collection. However, many designers secure financial support or backing for their catwalk shows, which are seen as essential in building a designer's business or brand.

All fashion shows follow a similar process in production, the variables being budget and scale. The budget must allow for venue, models, music, hair, make-up, show producer, ticketing and promotion. Costs tend to be high and planning is exhaustive as shows are typically 'live' and scrutinised by the press, buyers and fashion experts. Decisions

3

2

have to be made on each aspect of the production and invariably there are problems that demand patience and flexibility. At this stage of the process deadlines become critical, as the show will be scheduled for an exact time and date and rehearsals are required to ensure that the models have time to change and also understand any choreography requirements.

The collection will usually be shown as looks, or exits, where each piece is coordinated to present the designer's vision. Larger collections will be shown by colour, fabric or occasion. Shows usually last about half an hour, depending on the number of looks or exits.

1–2 Catwalk presentation of graduate collection by Alison Gaukroger.

3 Make-up artist Vaida Mygnete with model backstage.

The team > **Showing the collection** > Giles Deacon

Giles Deacon, fashion designer, interview

1

2

How do you start your collections?
We start the next collection before we finish the one we are working on. For example, the autumn/winter 2009 research started three weeks before the spring/summer 2009 show. We need to keep up the pace in the studio as certain staff are on a monthly salary, so we are producing all the time and do pre-collections as well. When researching for the new collection I use stuff that has been collected all year round and I work in sketchbooks.

How do you develop new shapes?
Patterns that haven't worked in the past are reworked. Cutters work on new shapes from inspirational mood boards; finishes may come from any surplus garments for new fabrics. I also set mini projects for assistants and students who will go around the shops looking at how garments such as those at Prada and Lanvin are made. The interpretations of new styles need to look like they come from Giles.

How many collections do you design?
There are eight in total: two main collections, spring/summer and autumn/winter for Giles; two pre-collections for July and November; and four collections a year for New Look.

How many are in your team?
There are nine full-time, four part-time and a number of students.

How do you compile a colour palette?
I do it instinctively, starting with core black and navy and adding a few new colours for trims. Choosing a colour is not a major problem.

Where do you source your fabrics?
Japan and the UK, France for denim, lace from Austria and I develop crêpe fabrics in UK mills who will produce 30 metres specifically for us.

How do you develop your prints and knitwear?
I have a long working relationship with designers Fleet and Rory, who interpret the feel of the collection or prints. Ideas develop in conjunction with the print designers. Rory works through drawings and Fleet works texturally. Syd will work large-scale knitwear showpieces and fine gauge knitwear samples are made in Italy. We also use Swarowski crystals on embroideries and prints.

How do you communicate with your cutters?
I sketch ideas for our creative cutters who work on patterns and draping on the stand. They draw in cloth on the stand, working spontaneously putting things on and often create happy accidents that are made into toiles for the collection. We photograph everything and keep notebooks.

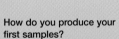

3

4

**How do you produce your
first samples?**
All samples are made in the studio
and if I am travelling, the team will
send images of development
samples by phone.

**What do you define as a range
within a collection?**
Little families. I use a range grid
which gives me an overview, for
example 70 per cent dresses, ten
per cent coats, ten per cent skirts
and ten per cent tops.

How much do your dresses sell for?
They start at £600 ($950) and go up
to £2,000 ($3,200) in the department
stores. Everything we show is for
sale. A special one-off gown sold in
Barneys or La Moda can go for
£30,000 ($48,000).

How many looks do you show?
About 42, with the first ten looks
setting the feel of the show.

**Do you collaborate with
anyone else?**
Yes, Stephen Jones for the hats,
Christian Louboutin for shoes. Also
LCF, Swarovski and MAC are
sponsors. I also work with Dell Intel,
LG Phones, Tanqueray No. Ten and
CPL perfumes.

Do you work with a stylist?
Yes, Katie Grand. We have meetings
throughout the season and finalise
colours and fabrics together.

Where do you sell your collection?
We have a showroom in Paris
to show to store directors and
head buyers for two weeks after
the shows.

1–4   Illustrations by
       Giles Deacon.

Shelley Fox, fashion and textiles designer, interview

1–2

How do you start your collections?

My collections don't start with a blank sheet of paper. With the Philadelphia Florist, I found three diaries in a flea market and lived with them for three years; then, when a fellowship came up at the Stanley Picker Gallery at Kingston University, I thought the diaries could be used for the project. I am constantly collecting things but I don't always know when and where I am going to use them. I never dump an idea once the collection is done as ideas will go somewhere else in the future. I think there is a constant thread of interest weaving its way through each collection, with a different point of view depending on how you are feeling at the time. In 1998 I produced my first installation, called the Braille collection, which became an iconic collection in the Joseph store during London Fashion Week. It has since been shown in a number of international exhibitions; most recently in the exhibition called 'Archaeology of the Future' by forecasting guru Li Edelkoort, in Paris and Eindhoven.

How many collections do you design?

Now that I am located in New York, and working around my professorship at Parson's, I could only manage one project a year or over a longer period. I think it is still important for me to develop my own way of working. I stopped producing collections to sell in 2004. The next big project after that was 'Fashion at Belsay', an installation that was staged in a 19th century house in Northumbria, England. It was based around clothing but as packed walls rather than mannequin displays.

Do you compile a colour palette and, if so, how?

I am not an overly colourful collection designer as I tend to focus more on silhouette and texture, but there have been collections where I have worked with scorched yellow wools, morse-code-printed fabrics and burnt sequin fabrics. Colour is not a priority at the beginning of a collection. The all-white Philadelphia Florist collection came about from a white fabric I sourced from a company in Japan; it was more about fabric manipulation than print.

How and where do you source fabrics?

A combination of Première Vision for good basics such as great suitings and shirtings from the UK. I have developed an identity for making my own fabrics, such as felting from my graduation collection, using yarn supplied by John Smedley, knitted at Nottingham Trent and felted in washing machines. For production I train assistants in the felting process to know the right handle. No two garments are the same in production and the beauty is in the uniqueness.

Do you commission textiles, such as knit, print, weave and embroidery?

I have worked with knitwear designer Tomoko at Livingstone Studios for chunky hand-knits when she was still at the Royal College of Art. She worked on a couple of collections for me. I also worked closely with Todd and Duncan who sponsored yarns for three seasons and then the clothing was produced in a factory in Hawick, Scotland.

3

How do you develop your
shapes and silhouettes:
flat pattern, draping or
modelling on the stand?
The early circle cutting was based
on cutting up crude drawings to
create new silhouettes. It was a
process that developed over some
early collections; it was influenced by
my partner who is a fine artist and
has a different head on my work.
Shapes are also developed on the
stand and then photographs taken of
the details; the design is developed
back and forth between drawing and
photography and eventually we work
on the cutting. Once the fit is right on
the stand the shapes are then made
into a flat pattern.

How do you create your first
samples and how many are
made for each collection?
First samples are made in the
studio but the knitwear goes out to
be sampled in the factories straight
from spec sheets, which have
already been sampled in toile form
in the studio. For my own label,
agents used to select samples
from Japan that were relevant to
them and they were remade.

How many looks on average per
collection are for catwalk only?
I made 12 outfits for my MA
collection at Central Saint Martins
but I have done up to 45 outfits,
which can cost too much money to
repeat in different colours and fabrics
for production. The collections were
often confusing when they got too
big. I keep the best press pieces
and usually a copy of each piece
for archive and sell the rest through
sample sales.

Do you have any second
lines to the main range?
No, as I never really designed the
collections that way. It was more
important for me to focus on the
main collection.

How do you work with stylists
and PR for selling the collection?
I have worked with different stylists
in the past such as Nancy Rhode
and, more recently, Jane Howard for
the Spectres show at the V&A. I also
worked with Abnormal PR – they
held each collection for six months
to show to press and worked with
me closely on the shows.

1–3 Shelley Fox's Philadelphia
Florist exhibition at the
Stanley Picker Gallery,
Kingston University.

Richard Nicoll, fashion designer, interview

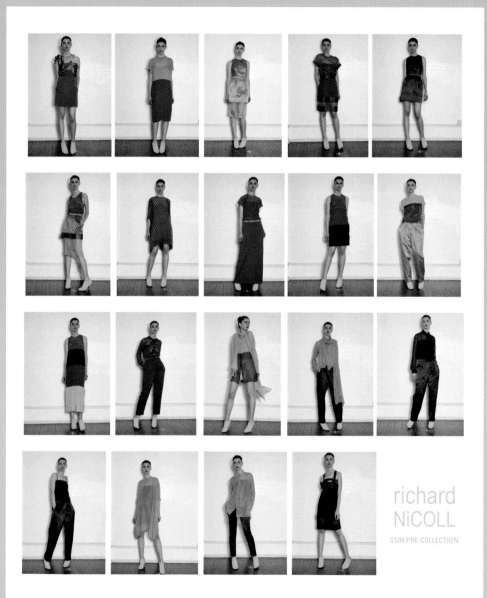

richard
NiCOLL

SS09 PRE-COLLECTION

What was your first collection after graduating?
After freelancing for other companies (Topshop, Matthew Williamson and Bora Aksu) and assisting stylists, Mandi Lennard PR asked me to do a small capsule collection of eight dresses for autumn/winter 04 called 'Twisted'. This was developed from my graduate collection, which was sporty with engineered panelling based on couture techniques. Lulu Kennedy at Fashion East saw it and sponsored the winter version, which included jackets. I met my business partner who turned my spring/summer 06 collection into a reality and sold it to b Store in London. I did three New Generation shows, which were unprecedented; one of them was a slide show, which was a collaboration with a stylist.

How do you start your collections?
I start with silhouette, then research, which starts with mood then colour palette. I produce a basic toile that informs a few outfits. I design the components separately, such as five ideas for five bottoms, then sleeves separately, so that pieces build up. I then draw the outfits in line-ups.

How many collections do you design?
I design two collections twice a year and two pre-collections.

How many are in your team?
There are four cutters, one for tailoring, and I work with Jacob, who is a stylist.

How and where do you source fabrics?
I source fabrics from stock that mills carry and also agents, such as an Italian agent that carries specialist silks from Tessio and I use fabrics from Canepa in Switzerland for shirtings.

Where do you produce your samples?
I have them made in factories in Poland and France for tailoring and dresses; shirts are made in England.

How many pieces on average per collection are for catwalk only?
About 10–15 per cent are for catwalk only and are couture pieces.

How many pieces/exits are in each collection and does this vary by season or line?
It can be anything from 23 outfits to 39 (which was the last collection and too many); usually about 35 for the main collection, with fewer in a pre-collection.

How many second lines to the main range do you have?
I design a range for Thomas Pink, which started out with shirts and has now moved into dresses (I have done a photo shoot using model Ben Grimes, which is very different for them). I also design a range for Designer Collaborations at Topshop. I also do a shirt range called Richard Nicoll Shirt for Barneys in New York.

Do you collaborate with other sponsors or brands?
I work with Christian Louboutin on shoes, Serapian for bags and Ksubi for sunglasses. I do the entire look with the running order, including accessories. My hats for the collections are made by Jeffrey Pullman.

1   Look book of S/S09 pre-collection by Richard Nicoll.

Markus Lupfer, fashion designer, interview

**How do you start
your collections?**
I go to Première Vision to look
for fabrics with an idea of something
I have researched before. I find new
things, developments in fabrics, then
do more in-depth research looking in
libraries and markets for themes
and inspiration. Researching is
24-hour looking, with fresh ideas
every season.

**How many collections
do you design?**
Four: two seasonal collections
for Armand Basi in Spain and two
for my own label Markus Lupfer in
London. For pre-season ranges
I will have a core range and add
embroidery or dip-dye for a
flexible service.

**Do you compile a colour
palette and, if so, how?**
After Première Vision I decide on
colourways to sample, depending on
the season, but I always keep it open
because fashion is a chameleon and
it is important to change with how
you feel and bring in personal soul.

**How and where do you
source fabrics?**
Italy, France, Germany and Japan.
I also go to Moda In, a fabric fair in
Milan, but it is not as important as
Première Vision. I also visit agencies
and specialist mills.

**Do you commission textiles: knit,
print, weave and embroidery?**
Knit and jersey for Markus Lupfer
and knit, jersey, woven and leather
for Armand Basi. I give research
inspiration to knitters and embroiderers
to develop things in the season; if
commissioned too far ahead things
may change within the collection.
I source embroideries in India for
Armand Basi and in Hong Kong
and the UK for Markus Lupfer.

**How do you develop your shapes
and silhouettes?**
Before and after Première Vision
I will collect a file of initial ideas and
tear sheets to create a library; this
is where the 'pyramid' starts. The
pyramid represents the ideas being
refined and edited right up until the
final collection, which is the peak.

For my own collection I start with
flat patterns, then modelling on the
stand and back to flat patterns.

**Where do you create your first
samples and how many for
each collection?**
Samples for Markus Lupfer are
made in London; for Armand Basi
they are made in the factory in Spain.
For Armand Basi I have to draw up a
range plan of first designs early on as
it is a ready-to-wear line and I need to
provide all the designs as accurately
as possible. Only during the fittings
can I change styles. If a look is not in
place I will have to drop it so that I can
focus on the range plan of designs
going into the collection. The range
will consist of coats, jackets, trousers,
dresses, tops and skirts. About 8–10
dresses will be in the final collection
depending on the season.

**On average, how many looks per
collection are for catwalk only?**
For Armand Basi usually about 35,
which are approved by their PR.

**How many looks are there in
each collection?**
For Armand Basi looks vary and can
be between 125 and 150 pieces for
each collection. For Markus Lupfer
there are 70 pieces in each
collection. For jersey they include
tops, dresses, trousers and
skirts, and for knitwear they include
dresses, tops and cardigans.

**How many second lines to the
main range do you design?**
Markus Lupfer for Topshop only.

**Do you collaborate with other
sponsors or brands?**
I have collaborated with Kangol,
Mulberry, Ruffo and Cacharel with
Clements Ribeiro, who I used to
work for. I don't have any
particular sponsors.

**How do you edit and present
the collections to your clients?**
Through my PR for Markus Lupfer
and with a stylist for Armand Basi.

**Where do you sell your
collections?**
I sell in Japan and Germany. I am
going to be selling the Markus Lupfer
knitwear and jersey pieces online for
ASOS, which is very exciting.

**Any advice for graduates
who want to design their
own collections?**
You have to be determined and have
to love it. If you are not 100 per cent
about it then don't start!

1   Markus Lupfer resort
     collection 2009.

Richard Nicoll > **Markus Lupfer** > William Tempest

William Tempest, fashion designer, interview

1

How do you start your collections?

I usually start by visiting libraries, sourcing images and looking at how clothes are worn. My ideal woman would be someone like Charlotte Rampling; intelligent and interesting, not a glitzy person. I prefer to think about real women, and this influences my own design style.

How would you describe your design style?

Evening wear, glamour with a twist. Comfort is important. I check the fit myself with the models and listen to their comments as the garments are being developed. I don't like to design for stick-thin women.

You graduated in 2007 – how did you get to this stage so quickly?

During my time at college I had worked at Giles on placement and continued this during my final year. I spent one season at Giles when I graduated. Whilst at college I won a scholarship, sponsored by Marchpole, in London. Marchpole has links with Jean Charles de Castelbajac in Paris, which led to an interview and the offer of a position there. I was one of Monsieur de Castelbajac's assistants. It was great and I learned a lot. In France, the employment law means that after three months the contract can be extended towards a permanent position, which is what the company planned. Living in Paris was great

and the company had arranged an apartment for me, but at the point where my contract was going to be extended, I was contacted by a company in the UK who had seen my work at the degree show. The company were interested in working with me, to back me as a designer. I decided this was a great opportunity, and returned to London to pursue this collaboration.

How did you start your own label?

I approached a number of organisations to find out more about support and showing in London. My backer has financed a show for me and is happy for me to develop my own range in this way, whilst working with them.

How did you develop this new collection?

It's a spring/summer collection, and I started by looking at my graduate collection – glamour with an edge or twist. I went to Harvey Nichols and Selfridges to look at price points for similar fashion – commercially viable pieces. Then I went to Première Vision in Paris for fabric sourcing; I had made a number of contacts whilst at Giles, so that was really helpful. I'm working on 12 outfits for this collection.

Is it tough doing everything yourself, in terms of managing it all?

Well, it's about 40 per cent creativity and 60 per cent business and managing. Total organisation is required to make it work. I produce weekly plans to ensure that everything is going to schedule. Working for Giles and Castelbajac was invaluable too – hands-on experience in how a business works.

1–2   A/W08 collection by William Tempest.

2

Colin McNair, menswear designer at John Varvatos, interview

1–3

How do you start your collections?

We start with the colour palette and then usually go to vintage appointments in London, Paris and New York and collect new pieces we like. This kicks off a mood, feeling or look, along with what John Varvatos himself is thinking and his direction. We will also be reading magazines for looks, proportions and ideas; we try to visualise what we want to achieve. We will look at vintage patterns for shirt and tie layouts, knit and sweater swatch suppliers for stitches and patterns. Along with this we will start to look at fabrics for all categories at fabric fairs and suppliers we work with each season. We will discuss as teams what we are thinking and bounce ideas off each other. Based on all the above I will also start to play with graphic ideas for T-shirts and begin working with graphic designers. We also look at past seasons and build SKU (single kimbled unit) plans in terms of how much we developed last season and what was actually sold. We have meetings with sales teams to discuss good sellers and bad sellers, meet with retail stores to get feedback and talk to customers.

How many collections do you design?

We design four collections a year – resort, spring, pre-fall and fall. Each collection is approximately 120 pieces, which does not include all the colourways and different fabrications we offer. It's big!

How many are in the design team?

There's John (CEO of the company), who is heavily involved in design. I have four designers for the younger line: one for wovens (outerwear, jackets, shirts, pants); one for denim and casual; one for knits and sweaters; and an assistant. I oversee a team of technical designers who work on specifications and fitting, commenting through development and production stages. I also work with one graphic designer. The main collection line has four designers on wovens, three designers on knits and sweaters and one for accessories. They are also supported by technical design.

Do you compile a colour palette and, if so, how?

This is the first thing we do. We collect colours I like and images of colour and start putting them together in a way that fits with season and inspiration. We have a colour library of old fabric swatches, pantones and yarns that we pull from.

How and where do you source fabrics?

Fabric/yarn fairs such as Milano Unica, Première Vision and Pitti Filati and trips to Asia and Europe where we visit mills and look at their collections (we also have the mills visit us in the office). We mainly use fabrics from Asia (China, Korea and Japan) and Italy.

Do you commission textiles: knit, print, weave and embroidery?

We don't commission as such. We buy vintage shirtings from vintage suppliers and put them into work with our weavers and printers. I buy sweater stitches and patterns from knit designers.

How do you develop your shapes and silhouettes: flat pattern, draping, modelling on the stand?

We design the clothes and send out technical packs to factories to follow for making the first prototype. Technical packs consist of all designs, detail sketches, specs, materials and all the information a factory needs to construct a garment. We usually have old styles to refer to for fit, on which we base new styles. If it's a new factory or a new fit we usually try to send an example from past seasons or a vintage garment to copy.

1–5   Illustrations by Colin McNair for John Varvatos.

4–5

Where and how do you create your first samples? How many approximately are made for each collection?
A lot! The first stage is the most experimental, so we put a lot of work into this to see what looks best. We cancel things when we see them if they don't look good and that's generally how we edit down to what we sample/show to buyers. First samples are made from the tech packs we send out. We then get a first prototype back and fit/comment on it. We send these comments back to the factory and they proceed to make a sample in the correct fabric with all the correct trim, wash and finishing. If we are on time or we feel we need to see it again, we make a second prototype before making the actual sample.

What do you define as a collection or a range?
A group of clothes that can consist of different categories, such as outerwear, leather, pants, jackets, denim (jeans), shirts, knits, sweaters and accessories.

How many pieces on average per collection are for catwalk only?
None: the catwalk is taken directly from the designed collection.

How many pieces or exits are in each collection and does this vary by season or line?
Yes it varies. I find the more focused and edited the collection, the better it sells. We usually develop and sample the collection, which is then edited by sales by 30 per cent. They sell the edited selection and then usually find the collection is edited by a further 20 per cent as some things don't sell. We cannot predict what buyers will buy and you have to offer a selection.

How do you present the collections to your clients?
The sales team sells the collections from our showrooms, which are in-house also.

How do you work with stylists, marketing and PR for selling the collection?
Stylists work with John to style the show. After the show, the collections will be sold by the sales team and after selling season, the collections then go to PR who send out to magazines, photo shoots and clients for selling and promotions.

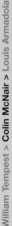

Louis Armadola, chief merchandising officer at Brooks Brothers, interview

How do you start your collections?

We are not a fashion-forward company but we are customer driven. First we analyse how product lines perform, what sold and why, such as fit of garment. We study trading reports and are influenced by the sales history, for example a dress season can affect the sales of skirts. Secondly, we will be inspired by archive designs from 190 years of trading as a heritage brand. Thirdly we are influenced by global trends. The design team will visit Première Vision and catwalk shows to get trends and forecasts together with looking at the history of Brooks Brothers.

How many collections do you design?

We have four major deliveries in our main range: fall, holiday, spring and summer. We have two deliveries in fall and only one in summer. A delivery can be from 100 to 200 styles. For Thom Browne, current guest designer on the Black Fleece range, we have two collections each with 50 styles in total.

How many are in the design team?

Ten in total led by the creative director, with guest designers for specialist ranges, such as Thom Browne for the Black Fleece range, Junya Watanabe for a reinterpretation of the classic Brooks Brothers button-down shirt range. Designers work as part of a three-pronged attack: merchant plus designer plus product developer.

Do you compile a colour palette?

We use classic colours for our foundation palette supplemented by colours from trend services, Première Vision and Pitti Filati. Our V-neck sweater for men will be produced in 30 colours.

How and where do you source fabrics?

Up to 50 per cent are sourced in Italy, the remainder from Japan.

Where do you make your first samples?

The first samples are made in the factories where they are produced. Tech packs are produced by the technical department, who also produces patterns and first samples. We also have a tie factory, where fabrics are sourced from Italy and England.

How do you produce new shapes and silhouettes?

The design team develops new shapes based on existing styles. The process evolves rather than producing revolutionary new shapes; for example slim-fit shirts, if the trends are for a slimmer silhouette.

Do you commission knit, print and embroideries for the collections?

Knitwear is sourced from outside services, based on sketched details. Prints are designed from our own archive.

1   Vintage advertising for Brooks Brothers.

How many second lines do you produce?

Brooks Brothers has a manufacturing division for uniforms for hotels, airlines and the military.

How do the designers communicate their ideas for the new collections?

They work to a designer brief which is a road map for the direction of the collection. They will work closely with the merchants for styling and sampling. The designs then go into work in the form of samples. They are taken to an adoption meeting where designers and merchants will work for days putting together the collection of 50 styles that will be bought for the stores.

How do you promote the collection?

We spend 50 per cent more than other companies in advertising and promotion. We produce a catalogue and look book to promote each collection. The Brooks Brothers customers are loyal to the brand and feel part of the family. We have store events and email customers for their feedback. Brooks Brothers is known as the place you were taken to for your first blazer, so there is a sentimentality associated with the brand, similar to Tiffany & Co., representing generations of style.

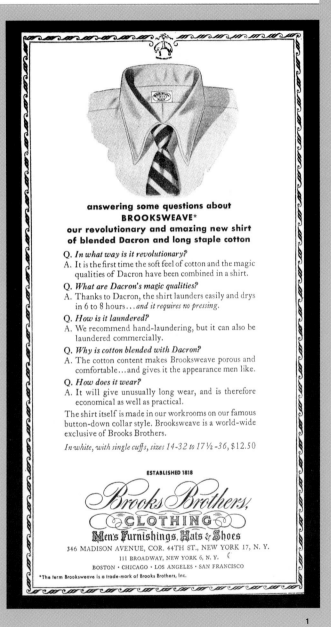

answering some questions about
BROOKSWEAVE*
our revolutionary and amazing new shirt
of blended Dacron and long staple cotton

Q. *In what way is it revolutionary?*
A. It is the first time the soft feel of cotton and the magic qualities of Dacron have been combined in a shirt.

Q. *What are Dacron's magic qualities?*
A. Thanks to Dacron, the shirt launders easily and drys in 6 to 8 hours...*and it requires no pressing.*

Q. *How is it laundered?*
A. We recommend hand-laundering, but it can also be laundered commercially.

Q. *Why is cotton blended with Dacron?*
A. The cotton content makes Brooksweave porous and comfortable...and gives it the appearance men like.

Q. *How does it wear?*
A. It will give unusually long wear, and is therefore economical as well as practical.

The shirt itself is made in our workrooms on our famous button-down collar style. Brooksweave is a world-wide exclusive of Brooks Brothers.

In white, with single cuffs, sizes 14-32 to 17½-36, $12.50

ESTABLISHED 1818

Brooks Brothers,
CLOTHING
Men's Furnishings, Hats & Shoes
346 MADISON AVENUE, COR. 44TH ST., NEW YORK 17, N. Y.
111 BROADWAY, NEW YORK 6, N. Y.
BOSTON · CHICAGO · LOS ANGELES · SAN FRANCISCO
*The term Brooksweave is a trade-mark of Brooks Brothers, Inc.

1

Colin McNair > Louis Armadola

'I am not just making a dress, I am telling a story. While the dress is important it's just one part of the story.'

Ralph Lauren

It is possible to group or identify common themes in fashion, those which influence the creative process in developing a collection, or how we choose to wear clothes. Recurring influences include traditional costume, active sports, workwear, the military, politics and futurism.

Each new collection can explore a subtle redefinition of these recurring influences through the use of colour, fabrics, proportion and juxtaposition. Many designers establish successful brands based on a visual identity that celebrates a particular theme. This chapter provides some examples of designers' sources and influences in designing collections. Although by no means an exhaustive list, it illustrates how designers respond to influences and translate them into a fashion reality reflecting their own design identity. It does not seek to identify consumer groups or particular fashion tribes or subcultures, but focuses instead on some of the sources of creative fashion and those designers renowned for defining a particular identity or style.

Background

1   Vivienne Westwood in iconic tartan bondage suit c.1977.

2   Martin Margiela A/W02. Catwalking.com.

Every season, designers strive to develop their signature look or visual identity through their collections. Often they reference a number of sources and influences relevant to the current political and social climate. For example, the emergence of deconstruction and reconstruction is evident during times of recession, such as in the early 1990s and during the economic downturn of the late 2000s. New, radical directions in fashion are often a reflection of, or a reaction to, the excesses of the time.

Vivienne Westwood transcends all influences and themes with her iconic collections. During high unemployment in the UK in the early 1970s, she and partner Malcolm McLaren were instrumental in launching the aggressive 'uniform' of the anti-establishment punk movement. Her use of tartan is legendary, from the early bondage trousers to the exquisite tailoring of recent collections.

1

The glamorous, hedonistic, luxurious look of the 1980s was led by Italian designer Gianni Versace, the 'King of Excess'. This upwardly mobile period in fashion allowed women to 'dress for success'. Of course, other designers reacted to these excessive styles. Rei Kawakubo's Comme des Garçons collection caused a strong negative reaction in the early 1980s: her startlingly avant-garde, all-black collection in Paris was famously called 'Hiroshima Chic' by the press. The Antwerp Six and Martin Margiela were inspired by this reactionary approach to design and their unique methods of deconstruction continued to influence fashion throughout the 1990s: a direct reaction to the excesses of the time.

The Antwerp Six
'A gang of fresh new fashion talents is determined to put Belgium on the map.' *Elle* USA, 1988.

The original six designers to bring Belgian fashion to the forefront were Dries Van Noten, Ann Demeulemeester, Dirk Bikkembergs, Dirk Van Saene, Walter Van Beirendonck and Marina Yee, who all graduated from the famous Antwerp Academy of Fine Arts. The strict four-year training, with its origins in Parisian haute couture, encouraged them to look inward on a journey to self-expression. According to their course director Linda Loppa, 'the designers were all original but shared the same perfectionism.'

Martin Margiela
A contemporary of the Antwerp Six, Margiela also graduated from the Antwerp Academy of Fine Arts. He launched his label Maison Martin Margiela in 1988 and since then has challenged the fashion world with his conceptual approach and presentation of collections. He is famous for not giving interviews. Even the store uniform is avant-garde – white lab coats make staff look like they work in a cult laboratory.

Conceptual influences

The origins of contemporary, conceptual fashion may well be credited to the Japanese designers Rei Kawakubo, Yohji Yamamoto and Issey Miyake. For decades, these designers have been producing the most intriguing, provocative fashion by creating new ways of cutting and constructing. Conceptual collections are often beautiful, timeless, ageless and dislocated from most visual narratives; however, they can also be too challenging, abstract or unrelenting in identity, diminishing their influence on fashion trends. Designers Hussein Chalayan, Helmut Lang and Jil Sander are all known for a minimalist, exacting aesthetic, which owes much to the rigours and precision of innovative architecture and reductive product design. There is usually little or no decoration to obscure the essence of the proportions, cut, finish or quality of fabrics used. Beauty derives from the garments' core components and construction.

1

> **'Hussein Chalayan is not just a fashion designer. His interests range across many disciplines; his work crosses so many boundaries.'**
>
> Donna Loveday

2

Hussein Chalayan

Hussein Chalayan trained as an architect before studying fashion at Central Saint Martins, London. He is known for his conceptual collections and intellectual approach: for example, he buried his graduate collection to see how it would decompose. Chalayan's collections reflect his explorations into product design and aircraft engineering: he created a jumbo jet dress that spread its wings and has made dresses grow and disappear through technology. One of his most famous collections was

'Afterwards' of autumn/winter 2000, which featured a set of 1950s furniture in a white room. The models dressed in the furniture covers and a wooden table transformed into a skirt; this has since become an iconic statement of Chalayan's conceptual aesthetic.

1   Jil Sander A/W08. Creative director Raf Simons (who originally trained in technical design) has continued the label's conceptual aesthetic. Catwalking.com.

2   Afterwards collection by Hussein Chalayan, A/W00. Catwalking.com.

Background > Conceptual influences > Form and function

Form and function

1   Christopher Bailey for
    Burberry Prorsum A/W08.
    Catwalking.com.

2   Original poster advertising
    early Burberry uniforms.

3–4 New designer Sophie
     Hulme references military
     influences to create her
     luxury sportswear pieces.

Functional garments, such as military wear and expedition clothing, have long influenced fashion designers. Menswear in particular continues to reference iconic military garments, workwear and utility clothing, being updated in fabric, colour and details.

Military clothing has informed fashion partly due to the performance and ergonomic considerations of the wearer's activities and environment, as well as its overall look. This consideration has attracted a number of designers, such as Robert Cary-Williams, whose army background influenced his earlier collections for colour and silhouette. Specifics such as camouflage have created an entire fashion agenda, involving recolouration and reapplication in unexpected contexts. The outcome may be as simple as Calvin Klein showing a military-inspired parka worn over a neat, single-breasted suit, with a shirt and tie. This exemplifies how a number of designers derive their inspiration and have created influential and successful fashion brands.

1

Military or Naval Catalogue Post Free on request.

Service Outrigs
BURBERRY

Uniforms and Topcoats
ensure security, comfort and distinction at home or abroad.

Burberry cloths, being woven and proofed by special processes without rubber or other airtight agents, afford hygienic and efficient protection against wet or chill and prolonged resistance to hard wear.
Made in strong, yet lightweight, textures, suitable for every war zone.

During the War Officers' Service of Burberrys, Tielockens and Burberry Trench-Warms Cleaned and Re-proofed FREE OF CHARGE.

BURBERRYS

EVERY BURBERRY GARMENT BEARS THIS LABEL.

Officers' Complete Kits in 2 to 4 Days

The Burberry Outrig.
Consisting of Service Uniform, Cap and The Burberry Weatherproof, fulfils the Soldier's every need.

BURBERRYS Haymarket **LONDON** S.W./I
8 & 10 Boulevard Malesherbes PARIS; and Provincial Agents.

2

Often one item of clothing emerges and creates a new fashion descriptor. The safari jacket, the riding jacket, the cargo pant and the biker jacket are all examples of this type of fashion transition. Occasionally, a garment defines an entire fashion category of its own, such as the Barbour, a waxed cotton shooting/fishing jacket that has become an iconic fashion statement in its own right. Another example is the trench coat; British companies Aquascutum (who pioneered the first waterproof gabardine) and Burberry (who launched the first trench coat after clothing the British army during the First World War) continue to produce these traditional 'foul weather' garments but have updated them to satisfy today's fashion-conscious consumer. The trench coat is now considered to be a fashion wardrobe staple and has itself been the inspiration for jackets, dresses, evening wear and children's wear.

3

4

Workwear

The origin for this source and aesthetic is arguably Levi Strauss, who in the late 1800s created the first work overalls using twill cotton from Nimes, in France. This twill cotton – denim – has since been popularised by nearly every known designer and an infinite number of manufacturers across the world. In music, films, politics, youth culture and high-end fashion, denim is used as a basis upon which unlimited fashion stories can be created. The cloth's traditional construction details can be reworked with endless possibilities: it is ageless, global and accessible to every social group. When asked if there was a garment he wished he had created, Yves Saint Laurent answered 'the blue jean'.

1

Sportswear

In the early 1980s American designer Norma Kamali launched a fashion business celebrating the use of traditional sweatshirting as a fashion fabric. This proved successful at a time when exercise and healthier lifestyles were beginning to dictate a new style of clothing. Kamali recently revisited this type of fashion by collaborating with Everlast in the USA to design an extensive range of 'fashion sweats' for today's body-conscious woman. Around the same time in London, two British designers launched their Bodymap label, which was a reductive, loose style based on Californian sportswear.

The sports world has inspired a number of fabric and garment developments specific to athletic performance and associated activities. The international interest, appeal and support for modern sport has proven irresistible to designers and producers. Companies have been swift to collaborate with a number of fashion and product designers to raise consumers' awareness of sportswear as a credible, lifestyle fashion statement. For example, sportswear brand Puma has collaborated with designers such as Alexander McQueen. Fred Perry has worked with Comme des Garçons in refreshing the iconic sports polo shirt and Adidas has successfully created Y3 with Yohji Yamamoto, to include full catwalk presentation of this sportswear and fashion fusion.

1 Fashion denim range by Poppy Dover.

2 Menswear collection by Peter Perrett, influenced by traditional sportswear and classic functional garments.

2

Futuristic influences

The US designer Geoffrey Beene is regarded as a futurist: in the late 1990s he decided to no longer use historical references on the basis that too many designers over-depend on them, restricting their development as innovative designers. He was responsible for redefining modern womenswear as we know it today.

In the 1950s and 1960s French designer Pierre Cardin, along with his contemporaries André Courrèges and Paco Rabanne, designed futuristic, space-age fashion, which referenced science fiction rather than historical and traditional sources. Futuristic fashion can be obvious in its presentation (such as 'space-age' clothes) but, more importantly, it is about breaking new ground, taking fashion in a new direction. For example, Cardin was the first couturier to launch a ready-to-wear line and he was subsequently expelled from Chambre de Syndicale in Paris. This represented the future of fashion as reflected by the demands of society. Similarly, a few decades earlier

1

2

1   Pierre Cardin's futuristic aesthetic.

2   Gareth Pugh's S/S09 collection had both futuristic and historical influences. Catwalking.com.

3   Viktor & Rolf A/W08. Catwalking.com.

in the 1920s, feminist Coco Chanel broke new ground when she emancipated women from the restricting corsets of the Edwardian period. Today's designers are no less radical. Menswear designer Aitor Throup creates his clothes from his exquisite illustrations. His work is futuristic in approach: he draws out the characters and converts them into a wearable version. By not focusing on design details he is freed up to produce a truly original final product. Gareth Pugh has evolved and refined the futuristic aesthetic displayed in his graduate collection. His exquisite pieces combine strong silhouettes and bold colour, which represent the future of fashion today.

3

Global influences

Since the 1960s international travel has become affordable and accessible to the majority of the developed world. This has greatly influenced our knowledge; how we can furnish our homes; choices in the foods we eat; and how we dress. Ever since Yves Saint Laurent first showed the Moroccan jellabah in the 1970s, designers and fashion consumers have understood the value and attraction of exotic, unusual garments, fabrics and accessories. Designers play with juxtaposition, colour or multicultural references; garments such as the Scottish kilt, Indian sari, Chinese cheongsam and Japanese kimono have been continuously redefined in fashion collections. Folklore and ceremony provides a wealth of information that can inform fabric design – such as tartan, ikat embroidery, paisley, prints and jacquards – as well as jewellery, footwear and accessories. Some designers have developed distinctive identities based on the celebration of international, cultural references for garments, fabrics, colour and surface decoration.

Two such examples are Kenzo and Dries Van Noten. Kenzo has championed the multicultural narrative, placing Russian floral prints, for example, alongside brightly coloured tartans and Norwegian snowflake knitwear graphics. Control of shape, silhouette and colour is a hallmark of Kenzo's work. The Kenzo style is clearly identifiable, influential and has remained constant for over 25 years. Dries Van Noten reworks ethnic influences, traditional textile techniques and colouration into the modern wardrobe. His love of ancient folklore and definition of adornment is carefully coloured from the sombre, urban uniform to the most colourful, embellished evening pieces using images and treatments inspired by a range of ethnic crafts. Internationalism, folklore and ethnicity continues to excite and contribute to many fashion collections. Examination of most designers' work will reveal the evidence of global influences.

2

Political influences

1

Fashion reflects society and designers will often reference political change in their collections. Messages through the clothes that we wear can be subversive or can be a bold statement to create a reaction. Katharine Hamnett famously did this when she invented the slogan T-shirt in the 1980s. These now iconic T-shirts were basic white with large, bold black lettering featuring socio-political messages such as anti-war statements. She intended for her slogans to be copied and read by people all over the world. Hamnett has now moved on to the global problem of ethics in the fashion manufacturing process; she is one of the designers responsible for introducing organic cotton to the masses.

Ethics and sustainability have become one of the main political agendas in fashion since the millennium. A number of designers have set up fairtrade and ethical labels, such as People Tree and 123, who publish manifestos to promote their beliefs. Larger companies are becoming influenced by emerging fairtrade organisations and are beginning to introduce their own ethical ranges.

Designers collectively have a common strength of purpose to challenge convention and break new ground in response to current affairs. For example, Alexander McQueen continues to reference topics such as war and religion in his memorable collections. He sets out to make his audience face certain issues, once featuring Aimee Mullins, a Paralympic athlete and model in his show. Jeremy Scott, whose first Paris collection was made of hospital gowns, also sets out to provoke people with his collections, which convey a message, an idea or a thought. Stella McCartney believes that fashion is political on a daily basis, that it is 'about people expressing themselves through what they choose to wear'. She is passionate about animal rights and refuses to include fur or leather in her collections. Jean Charles de Castelbajac uses political references in addition to his fine-art influences and translates these through humour in his colourful collections. His spring/summer 09 collection included a knitwear piece that featured an image of Barack Obama, the first African-American president of the USA; a bold statement that reflects the changes in American society.

1   In 1984 Katharine Hamnett famously met Margaret Thatcher wearing a political statement T-shirt.

2   Obama dress by Jean Charles de Castelbajac, A/W09. Catwalking.com.

Archivism

1   Matthew Williamson for
     Pucci. Catwalking.com.

2   Emilio Pucci at work,
     Florence, Italy in 1959.

3   1950s orange suit by
     Balenciaga.

4   Balenciaga S/S08.
     Catwalking.com.

In a fashion context, archivism refers to the way in which designers look back to previous collections for inspiration. In particular, the original aesthetic of a well-established label may be revisited decades later, with collections referencing the same design influences and detailing. For example, Italian nobleman Emilio Pucci was popular throughout the 1960s (and again during the 1980s) for his use of wild, colourful patterns taken from Renaissance paintings, filigree, feathers, animals, stained glass windows and ceramic tiles. He designed simple belted dresses, bodysuits, boatneck tops and pants in silk jersey. These iconic, bold prints continue to be referenced today, with creative directors such as Matthew Williamson bringing the label up to date for the modern consumer.

Another example is Nicolas Ghesquière at Balenciaga, who has continued Cristóbal Balenciaga's reputation to challenge the definition of aesthetics through a combination of strong silhouette, colour, proportion and fabrics. His interpretation of the founder's original vision has been internationally applauded as a considered way of redefining fashion; it is evidence that enquiry and intellectual content in fashion can be colourful and dramatically beautiful.

> *'He experimented with printing on velvet or towelling, weaving wool with ribbon, hemp with silk; constantly searching for better forms of stretch material. Pucci took textile technology as far as he could at the time.'*
>
> Valentine Lawford

3

4

Designers such as Karl Lagerfeld for Chanel and John Galliano for Christian Dior continue to reference the fashion houses' iconic statements, playing with scale, logos and accessories. These designers continue to update the signatures of the past in glamorous and sensationalist garments. There are many more designers who approach collections in this way, such as Jean Paul Gaultier at Hermès, Marc Jacobs at Louis Vuitton, Christopher Bailey at Burberry and Marco Zanini at Halston. These fashion sources fluctuate in importance and influence due to trend directions and fashion's ever-changing aesthetics. Many designers change direction from season to season or combine additional source materials and influences to refresh their signatures or styles. It is useful to see how other designers derive influences; it will in turn help to inspire you, and enable you to analyse and reflect on your own thoughts, preferences and creative identity.

James New, menswear designer at Vivienne Westwood, interview

How do you start your collections?

First a theme or mood is decided upon, whether it's abstract or real. It could be anything of interest or something that I would like to know about or learn. Another consideration is whether there is a message to be conveyed to the customer; this could be political, a current affair or theatrical or comical in some way. It is my belief that humour is very important in clothes. I want a man to look like a gentleman, a poet, a romantic, and have a sense of humour. This can be created in the clothes.

How many collections do you design?

I design two collections: the mainline collection, which is sold internationally and seen on the catwalks in Milan; and the Japanese licence collection, which is sold only to the Japanese market.

Do you compile a colour palette and, if so, how?

Colour palettes are vital for a collection; it is important to me to create a feeling of colours for each season. I look for colours everywhere, from any reference. I prefer to find fabrics and take the colour from scraps of cloth. Images from magazines and pictures are very helpful too. We are constantly surrounded by beautiful colours: in the city and the countryside, even when we walk to work. As a designer you should absorb as much information as possible as it will help you to get inspiration. I find too many people busy listening to their MP3 players and not appreciating what is going on around them; for me, the more you see and read the more ideas you gain.

How and where do you source fabrics?

Fabrics are sourced from Paris and Italy at fabric fairs. A great amount of time is spent sourcing fabrics through many different companies and after looking through fabric collections, orders for small cuts of fabrics are requested for anything which may be of interest at that time. Gradually relationships with particular companies are built up and you realise that you seem to favour certain companies over others and therefore you begin to disregard some. Especially in menswear you know which companies you need to see, those who do great wools and beautiful shirtings; but of course I am always on the lookout for new designs and structures in fabrics so it's vital to know what is new at the fabric fairs so that you are the first to find beautiful cloth.

How do you develop your shapes and silhouettes?

Shapes are developed in several ways. Sometimes I take an archive piece, which I am very fortunate to have in-house at the Westwood studios. These include all key pieces from previous collections; the archive dates back 30 years so it's full of ideas and shapes to rework. I can alter them and bring them to a more contemporary level and adjust them to be totally different garments by changing details, silhouette and of course the fabric. Flat patterns are used to make new shapes and ideas in three-dimensional form. Samples are made in calico and are then sent to the professional pattern cutters who use their more advanced skills to develop the sample to get the best shape. I am then able to see it made properly and alter it to my design taste if needed.

How do you produce samples and how many approximately are made each collection?

Samples are made in Italy at the factory for the mainline; sometimes up to 70 first samples are created so that each style can be viewed. For the Japanese licence, samples are created in Tokyo and about half the amount as for the mainline collections.

What do you define as a collection or range?

A collection for me is a story of clothes that reveal a theme or mood with the use of fabrics, silhouettes and shapes with colours and prints.

How many pieces are for catwalk only?

Four to six pieces are usually for catwalk only; these are called showpieces and they are only created for the theatre of a show but can be made for special order.

How many pieces/exits are in each collection and does this vary by season or line?

It changes a lot; there are many pieces and the collection gets bigger every season as sales increase. In the autumn/winter collections we have more coats and for the spring/summer collections we have a lot more jersey and T-shirts with prints, as one can imagine.

How many second lines to the main range do you have?

There is one other line, which is the Japanese Man licence. This is a collection designed for the Japanese taste and customer without losing the Vivienne Westwood image and feeling. It also caters for the Japanese body and sizes are created especially for them. It is intended to be a more commercial range than the mainline collection.

How many pattern cutters do you have and how do you communicate your designs to them?

There is one pattern cutter for each line, one in Italy and one in Japan. Communication of the designs is achieved by drawing on spec sheets and writing descriptions and measurements so everything is clear for them.

Do you do in-house reviews of the collections?

There are constant in-house reviews of the collections as they continue to be developed. There are meetings updating the design process to the production, as well as relaying the 'look' with the marketing department in order to increase profit every season. There are also talks with buyers and the press office to get feedback so that the customers are satisfied and new customers targeted for the future.

How do you present your collections to your clients?

I present collections to clients by doing a short presentation with the use of mood boards and garment samples. I talk about price points, fabric treatments, styles and the fabric itself; for example, the weight and quality and the composition of the fabrics.

How do you work with stylists, marketing and PR for selling the collection?

There is a close link with the marketing department to make sure garments are being created that the customer will want. There is good feedback on sales, which allows the best sellers and worst designs to be seen. This enables good decisions to be made on what to repeat and what not to do next season. By talking to the press and our directors I get

feedback on customers' comments and their view on what will make the collection stronger, for example what colours, fabrics and styles are performing well. It is very good for a designer to listen to the other team members from all departments so that more advanced designs and collections can be developed. Our design director Andreas Kronthaler does the styling for our collections.

1 Vivienne Westwood menswear A/W09. Catwalking.com.

1

Archivism > **James New** > Kenneth Mackenzie

Kenneth Mackenzie, fashion designer and founder of Six Eight Seven Six, interview

How do you start your collections?

My collections are personal and not largely defined but often use constant Six Eight Seven Six themes drawn from cultural and artistic influences. Six Eight Seven Six is always striving to go its own way and not be a slave to arbitrary trends and targets. Fundamentally, we aim to create clothing with design, longevity and quality. This guiding principle drives us to develop an evolving wardrobe reinterpreting the classical confines of menswear by blending the latest fabric and manufacturing technology with proven traditional materials and construction. Taking inspiration from art, music, idealism, architecture, product design and nature, we try and evolve an aesthetic that resonates with our lives and the lives of our customers. 'We' is an important concept at Six Eight Seven Six, for while we are built round a central core, we are in essence a collaboration, with a shifting cadre of artists and outsiders. We don't really do collections now, although we use the same influences for research.

How many collections did you design?

From 1995 to 1998 we did two collections a year for spring/summer and autumn/winter, which we wholesaled to stores. We started by finding garments, mainly workwear and military, such as army surplus from markets. We simplified the garments and took them into modern fabrication.

How did you source your fabrics?

We would go to Première Vision. It was restrictive finding fabrics. We were always trying to evolve new styles and even if we found a fabric five years after we first launched it, we didn't have the confidence to re-run a style years later. In the early days, we didn't want to leave Première Vision without all the fabrics but now we have become more relaxed and flexible in how we develop stuff. It is a good discipline to know your manufacturers and fabric mills to start with.

How many garments did you make?

When we went to Première Vision we took with us a collection in linear form of 20–25 pieces. We would find fabrics that would fit in two to three styles for minimum orders. Sometimes it didn't work because the factories found it difficult to make 25 styles in three different fabrics.

How did you develop shapes and silhouettes?

Our influences were always similar and still are: classic menswear with vintage sportswear. We were producing military with softer accessories, such as shoes with truckers at the end of the 1990s. Clothing became smarter so we did knitwear as a reaction.

When did you change how you develop your collections?

I had a break from my business, designed for A Life in NY and had a lifestyle change, bought a bike and went camping, then returned to the business in 2005. This time the ranges, rather than moderate collections, were more technical and mainly sportswear. The 2006/07 collection was based on geodesic domes with technical fabrics. Influences were also small-scale architecture in Japan with transient nature creeping into the house.

How many do you have in the design team?

I do all the design. I work with a stylist, Adam Howe, and have a photographer, Norbert.

Where do you produce your garments?

In factories in Portugal and Scotland. From the spring/summer 2008 samples we had worldwide orders so we cherry-picked a couple of existing styles and changed these to produce six styles. These were produced over three to four months. We removed the 'fillers', such as the knitwear and T-shirts to go under the jackets and concentrated on a few special pieces. We are focusing on what we do well, as we are a small company. We use five or six UK companies and one in Portugal for our manufacturing.

1   Pieces from the Six Eight
      Seven Six A/W06 range.

2   Six Eight Seven Six S/S06.

1

2

Do you collaborate with anyone?
We plan to collaborate with old-fashioned companies, such as Cleeve who supply Jermyn Street. We have sourced a vintage shirting from Japan at Première Vision, which we will use with a traditional British manufacturer to produce a fusion. There are certain technical processes that traditional factories won't do. We are also using finished products from Eastern Europe, particularly Slovakia, and then we modify them. The process is still vertical from fabric, trim, pattern to garment. We also collaborate with Folk clothing for technical styles, usually 200–300 pieces across two styles.

How do you sell and promote your ranges?
We produce a news bulletin for each style, showing the research, pricing, styling and technical changes. We still wholesale but stores pay upfront now. We have a personal relationship with buyers and the customers and we get instant feedback on our ranges for the next styles.

Sophie Hulme, fashion designer, interview

How do you start your collections?

I find stuff, old things I have collected and objects that I make into 3D garments, which I then sketch. I then design individual pieces rather than a whole look. I am not trend-led but I build a wardrobe of key pieces that are designed to last. Each season I develop a new trinket, which collectively will form a giant charm necklace.

How many collections do you design each year?

I design in two season brackets: autumn/winter and spring/summer, which are aesthetically different with signature pieces running through. I don't have a big fashion show but have seen buyers from the beginning with look books. Often they buy my pieces themselves, which is how my graduate collection was bought by Selfridges.

How many are in your team?

In my first season it was only me but for this season I have a freelance pattern cutter, a design assistant for specs and cutting, and some student helpers on work experience. I have a production manager for department store orders as I make to order and if the stock is delivered a day late the order can be cancelled.

How do you compile a colour palette?

I have a feeling about colour and usually have a base of neutrals with a few accent colours, such as greys with aubergine. Sampling is limited so I will swatch other colourways especially for buyers.

How and where do you source your fabrics?

I go to Première Vision in Paris and select stock fabric from mills and small companies in Italy, France and Korea. I buy between 50 and 100 metres and commission colours. I also visit Linea Pelle in Bologna to source leathers.

Do you commission your own textiles?

I design my own prints and have them printed in repeat; and I have fabric sequinned in India.

How do you develop your shapes and silhouettes?

I start working in 3D on the stand and don't use blocks.

How many samples do you produce?

I made 25 for the first autumn/winter season and 35 samples for spring/summer in a few colourways, as it is expensive to produce samples.

Do you have any sponsors or collaborate with anybody?

I have a PR called Cube but have no sponsors at present. I would like to collaborate with other people to produce special lines in future. I might possibly work in Japan with artists and go back to illustrating, which I only do for editorial at the moment.

Who are your stockists?

I showed at Rendez-Vous in Paris the first season, where Selfridges and b Store in London bought my collection. I will also have my collection in the Convenience Store in London.

1   Sophie's graduate collection featured military-inspired pieces, such as this sequin parka.

2   Illustration by Sophie Hulme.

Will Broome, fashion designer and illustrator, interview

How do you start your collections?

It varies from season to season. Working with a designer such as Marc Jacobs, they might ask what I am developing at the moment. It is an organic process and we collaborate through dialogue. There is a lot of time involved as we are working in partnership because they know and like my work. I have been collaborating on the Marc by Marc for six years. For autumn/winter 2004 I designed the multiple skull and panda prints for the womenswear collection and T-shirts for menswear. Then Wedgwood approached me to design their 250th anniversary china as they liked my style. They gave me carte blanche to work how I wanted. I felt it an honour to be asked by a heritage brand such as Wedgwood.

Describe your style of illustration

Cute with darkness behind: cutouts, naive, mainly in black and white. I don't use a computer to generate my work, only to scan. I choose to work with lack of precision and a return to the hand-drawn. I use paper stolen from the photocopier, pads of coloured paper and Berol fine liners (a red one for thick lines and turquoise for fine lines). I work in sketchbooks on the go and draw something every day. I used to get in trouble at school, but now I am a professional doodler!

How did you start?

I submitted A5 sketchbooks, which were used on the catwalk, the clothes, bags and stickers on everything.

How many illustrations do you produce per season?

Usually 25 drawings, maximum, which I collage to get a new image. Once they are sold they are exclusive to Marc Jacobs.

1–3   Illustrations by Will Broome.

1

2

Sophie Hulme > Will Broome

1   Haute couture dress by
Lanvin-Castillo, shown at
the Savoy Hotel, London
on April 1st 1957.

*'Above all it was Christian Dior who was my master
and was the first to reveal the secrets and mysteries
of haute couture.'*

Mark Bohan

Within the global fashion industry collections are designed
for various market levels. At each level it is important to
understand who the target customer is and how the collections
will be presented. To define the key areas of contemporary
fashion, the following market levels should be noted: haute
couture and bespoke tailoring, prêt-à-porter or ready-to-wear,
designer labels, luxury brands, high street or mass-market
brands and home shopping.

This chapter introduces each of these market levels,
discussing how the collections are developed and how the
design and development process differs at every level.

Haute couture

Haute couture is the highest, most specialist market level. Established houses such as Chanel, Givenchy, Gaultier, Dior and Lacroix are members of the Chambre syndicale de la haute couture and show their couture collections in Paris over three days in January and July. Currently there are only 12 full members compared with over 100 in 1946. Only garments that are hand made in France, by members of the Chambre syndicale de la haute couture, can be labelled as haute couture. But the Chambre may also invite guest designers, such as Martin Margiela, Valentino and Giorgio Armani, to show alongside other members in Paris. In 2008 Boudicca, the English design duo, were honoured with an invitation to show during Paris Haute Couture Week.

Chambre syndicale de la haute couture
This was the initiative of the first known English couturier Charles Frederick Worth. Couture houses that are members of Chambre syndicale de la haute couture must meet and maintain strict criteria, including specialist aspects of the manufacture process and the location. All processes are controlled within the atelier or studio (which may sometimes just be the artisans working in their own homes).

1

The origins of haute couture

The origins of haute couture can be traced back to the early 17th century, when France was the centre for luxury silk textiles in Europe. Aristocratic women would commission makers to produce personal gowns and accessories for social and court occasions. Makers, known as couturiers (from the French *couter* – to sew), would create one-off clothes for clients and include their names on labels sewn into the garments.

The atelier

Traditions continue with the couturiers of today. Within the atelier, which is usually owned by the design house, each garment type is created within a specialist area. The *flou* is an area specialising in dresses and draped garments. The *tailleur* focuses on tailoring for suits, jackets and coats. The chief dressmaker is known as the *première* and assistants are apprentices. Couture houses are traditionally separated by skills into the flou and tailleur. However, with more money to be made in daywear than evening wear, the boundaries are now blurring. For example, Karl Lagerfeld at Chanel commissions the dressmakers to work on unstructured jackets, which brings a lightness to the tailoring.

Couture gowns rely on the craftsmanship of the ateliers, where specialist handwork is carried out to the designer's and client's specifications. The atelier is the laboratory for developing and maintaining new fabrics, beading, cutting, embroidery and the highest level of handwork and finish. Chanel has bought five ateliers, including Lesage, which specialises in flowers, braids and feathers. Other houses in Paris, such as Dior, also use this atelier (Dior no longer owns its own specialist ateliers).

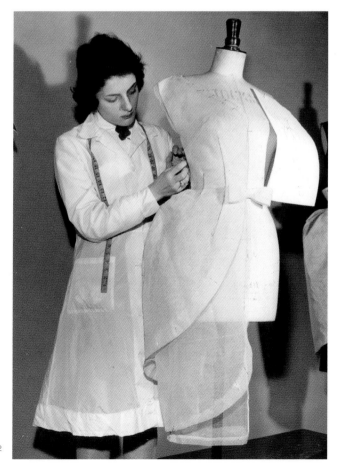

1   John Galliano for Dior haute couture A/W09. Catwalking.com.

2   Modelling on the stand.

Developing a haute couture collection

Designers begin haute couture collections in much the same way as ready-to-wear. John Galliano, for example, starts his haute couture collection by drawing sketches and selecting fabrics. Each season, showing the couture collection allows potential clients the opportunity to see first-hand the possibilities for next season's wardrobe. Appointments are then made with the designer/house to attend private viewings and make individual selections. Clients buy close to the season, seeing a show in January for that spring (unlike ready-to-wear, which shows for the following season). This ensures exclusivity for the client, who values the privacy and service only available at this level of the market. Then, after seeing the collection, a client will make an appointment with the *vendeuse* (saleswoman) in the salon. Having made a selection, the client must have the pattern adapted to ensure that the garments are personally fitted to their measurements and body proportions. A series of fittings will take place, using calico toiles. The toile records the exact cut, fit and finish and will also detail information for linings, interfacing and embellishments. The fittings and client selections are confidential and reflect the exclusive nature of this fashion market. Regular clients will, over time, have a personal form made to their exact measurements.

1 Chanel haute couture
S/S08. Catwalking.com.

Special occasions

Haute couture is aimed exclusively at women, with many of the clothes designed for events such as the Oscars ceremony in Los Angeles or the Cannes Film Festival in France. During these events the designers set up hotel workrooms to ensure that the client has fittings right up to the event.

The future of haute couture

Due to the extremely high costs associated with the production and purchase of couture clothing and the growth in popularity of ready-to-wear, there are fewer customers able or willing to buy couture. Many couture houses have closed their ateliers, although the label may continue in accessories or fragrances. In addition, changes in society mean that many social formalities have disappeared and so there is less demand for this type of clothing. It is estimated that there are approximately 300 women across the world who can afford to buy haute couture. As such, many designers and fashion houses will loan evening gowns to young celebrities to freshen the image of couture. Over the last 20 years a number of designers have expanded into this level of the market, including Versace, only to retreat when the cost and competition have proven to be unworkable or unnecessary to develop the core business.

1

Haute couture > Ready-to-wear

Ready-to-wear

Ready-to-wear, or prêt-à-porter, covers any collection that consists of garments produced in volume – distinct from the one-off garments in haute couture. Couture is establishment and classic, whereas ready-to-wear is young and subject to trends and change. A ready-to-wear collection is created for a wider customer base and will be produced in standardised sizes. Ready-to-wear can span from established design houses, who also produce couture, to international and smaller designers setting up independent labels.

The origins of ready-to-wear

Ready-to-wear in the USA
This can be traced back to the beginning of the 20th century, following the Industrial Revolution and the introduction of the sewing machine. Immigrants from Eastern Europe with tailoring skills settled in New York and set up workshops in crowded tenements to service the growing population. After the First World War, companies began to visit the Paris shows and buy patterns to copy for the American market using cut, make and trim outfits in New York. By the end of the Second World War this was replaced with licensing deals, which was less costly than buying couture samples to copy.

Couture houses first began to produce cheaper lines for their in-house boutiques in the 1930s. Then, after the Second World War, the couture houses established boutiques to cater for a changing world by offering off-the-peg collections, known as prêt-à-porter. These collections were based on their couture lines at an affordable price. Up until 1950, Italian and American fashions relied on Paris couture and highly skilled dressmakers would copy designs. Early forms of licensing were established by couturiers such as Christian Dior, who sold patterns and muslin toiles to the USA to be copied and sold in department stores.

After the death of Coco Chanel in 1971, Paris entered into a period of transition and the couture houses were struggling against mass production in the UK. The couture houses reacted by offering affordable, diffusion collections inspired by their couture styles. By the end of the 1970s the House of Chanel had launched its own ready-to-wear lines and Dior launched Miss Dior. Haute couture continued to influence the designer's ready-to-wear collections in fabric, colour, silhouettes and theme.

Many aspects of design and products were being reconsidered and exciting design ideas dispensed with existing aesthetics and materials. In the 1970s Yves Saint Laurent launched Rive Gauche – ready-to-wear for women and men. The Rive Gauche collections popularised his avant-garde approach to style, luxury and the contemporary fashion consumer. Based on the reputation of the hip Left Bank district of Paris, Saint Laurent created an enticing image of the modern consumer in touch with contemporary cultures – a global traveller who understood cultural and creative diversity and the courage to question convention. Saint Laurent successfully built an international fashion empire based on ready-to-wear whilst creating shocking (for their time) fashion statements, including the safari suit and 'Le Smoking' – a tuxedo-style suit for women. It could be argued that this look and many others from Saint Laurent provided the basic template for the modern women's wardrobe.

1   Yves Saint Laurent outside his new store in New Bond Street, London in 1969.

1

Luxury brands

The current fashion market covers product areas that extend far beyond clothing and personal accessories. Designers and retailers have created brands to define a lifestyle or design language that is communicated to consumers. As with other industries this creates a demand based on want rather than need. In today's world, there are trends in every aspect of life and we are all, to some extent, aware of what is fashionable.

Over the past 20 years, the designer ready-to-wear market has expanded to include an enormous range of labels, diffusion lines, accessories and other branded products. Pierre Cardin was the first designer to expand into a range of fashion and non-fashion areas. Cardin designed and branded eyewear, fragrances, Cadillac cars, footwear, telephones – even chocolates. This expansion was ultimately perceived as diminishing the brand, with the result that the Cardin name became devalued and unfashionable. Gucci suffered the same fate, coming to represent bad taste. Gucci re-evaluated their heritage and prior status by cancelling a large number of licences and by appointing Tom Ford as design director to refocus ready-to-wear. Following his first ready-to-wear collections in the mid-1990s Ford successfully repositioned Gucci as a global leader. His influence was used to redesign the Gucci store interiors, fragrance packaging and editorial campaigns – collectively refining the company's position as a luxury fashion house. When Yves Saint Laurent was sold to the Gucci group in 2000, Ford applied the same approach to reinvigorate the YSL brand – again with acclaim; he repositioned YSL at the forefront of modern ready-to-wear fashion.

Currently, international ready-to-wear designers have businesses aimed at different levels of the market. Regardless of market niche, each branded collection is created and produced in the same way. The brand is clearly identified as targeting specific customers or occasions, whilst aiming to capture the designer's identity either through design or advertising. Pricing, fabrics and finish are all used to differentiate each line.

International designers provide the main content for the ready-to-wear shows during Fashion Week in the fashion capitals of New York, London, Milan and Paris. In addition to the published schedules for these renowned shows, fashion weeks also take place across the world, in cities such as São Paolo, Melbourne, Shanghai, Tokyo, Madrid, Rome and New Delhi. The fashion industry is international in consumer awareness, demand, production and promotion, with brands such as Louis Vuitton, Gucci, Prada and Dior being recognised, demanded and available across the world.

2

1 Gucci A/W95. Tom Ford's first collection for Gucci redefined the luxury brand. Catwalking.com.

2 Futuristic dresses by Pierre Cardin.

Haute couture > **Ready-to-wear** > Mass market

1

Contemporary designers

1   Comme des Garçons S/S08.
      Catwalking.com.

2   'Blues' collection displayed
      in The Convenience Store,
      London.

This term is used to denote a group of younger, less internationally available designers, whom the media watch for future trend influences and the mass-market producers scrutinise and reproduce in an attempt to align their merchandise with key catwalk trends or looks. At times, the designer's look may be achieved through key accessories or by reworking garments to create a fresh or controversial fashion statement.

Contemporary designers will show twice a year either as part of the main ready-to-wear fashion week schedule or alongside these scheduled shows, which is known as 'off schedule'. Regardless of schedule details, these shows are often extremely popular, reflecting their exclusivity and limited distribution. Many of the collections shown by less-established designers are favoured by the press due to the significance of the show, either in terms of design or general direction or sometimes simply because of the outrageous clothes.

Collections by contemporary designers are usually sold through an international range of fashion specialist boutiques and concept stores such as Dover Street Market, Browns, b Store and The Convenience Store in London, Colette in Paris, Corso Como in Milan and Jeffrey in New York. These independent retailers specialise in selecting exclusive collections from international designers alongside up-and-coming labels, which creates a halo effect for new talent. The ultimate goal for small designer labels is to sell collections that they can produce, deliver and continue to supply.

Some designers are showmen who launch collections to attract major investors. Alexander McQueen did this and gained his first couture position at Givenchy. Gareth Pugh, whose graduate collection was theatrical and extreme, now produces exquisite collections backed by an Italian company, which enables him to show in Paris.

2

Mass market

Across many mass market or high-street retailers, each fashion collection or range is scheduled to be available in store at prescribed times. Known as 'drops', the collections will be staggered into early and high season. This 'fast fashion' offers the customer a changing retail experience, as subsequent items or stories will be delivered in a number of weeks. Most retailers will continue to offer core ranges that evolve from season to season, reflecting a more conservative customer or clothing area. Core ranges include men's suiting, separates and accessories. Nightwear, underwear and sweatshirt separates are also typical core lines – these are much less influenced by high-fashion trends or directions. Many retailers aim to offer new ranges every two weeks, although this merchandise strategy is mainly featured within fashion-focused retailers such as H&M and Topshop. New ranges are displayed in store as soon as delivery is received. The ranges are often promoted on the retailer's website or in the fashion press as news or 'buy it before it goes'.

Marks and Spencer

UK company Marks and Spencer, and the other high-street chain stores that followed, were not design innovators but suppliers of basic goods, much like US company Gap during the 1970s. Things began to change when head of design Brian Godbold employed Paul Smith as a design consultant. In the 1970s and 1980s the market became saturated with basic products, which in turn created a need for conspicuous design. M&S bought American brand Brooks Brothers in the 1980s, but didn't become an influence in fashion until the Autograph range was launched in 2000, which really changed the company's profile. Designers Betty Jackson, Julien MacDonald and Katharine Hamnett all designed upmarket capsule ranges that were to be sold anonymously under the Autograph label. M&S were also one of the first chain stores to support up-and-coming designers, funding Hussein Chalayan and Matthew Williamson for the New Generation show at London Fashion Week in 1998.

The supplier

Only a few chain stores have in-house design teams. They rely on the design teams employed by their suppliers or manufacturers and who are usually specialists in their core product, such as jersey or men's tailored trousers. As a result, the buyer will essentially 'design' or compile the collection by sourcing pieces from a number of suppliers. Increasingly, chain stores are using suppliers with factories in places where labour and fabric is cheap, such as Asia, South America and Eastern Europe. The buyers will begin with a base colour palette and mood boards to show their suppliers the intended theme for the collection. The suppliers will then provide samples and have weekly meetings with the buyers and merchandisers. Designers who work for suppliers have the opportunity to shop the world for sample garments.

1

In the UK, many factories were once 'vertical', which meant they produced both the cloth and the finished garments. However, most of the mills and factories have now closed down due to increasing costs and competition from mass production overseas. Some factories will be commissioned to produce a range of garments for the overall collection, but this is rare. One exception is Spanish retailer Zara, which is a vertical producer. The company's business structure enables production of both fabric and garments, thereby allowing for complete flexibility in production and styles. With its own retail outlets, Zara is able to control every aspect of the design, production and retail chain, whilst keeping costs in control and stock change responsive to fashion direction and sales. Stock is therefore planned to offer ongoing choice, with the customer aware that the items may be sold out in a few weeks. With the rapid and popular development of inexpensive, fast fashion, many consumers are now concerned about the ethics and sustainability of this market level. These concessions are being reflected in the emergence of retailers marketing eco-fashion as organic, fairtrade or socially responsible. This is a complex and challenging area for designers, manufacturers, retailers and consumers. But as an increasing number of environmental and social factors are demanding that we reconsider how and why we consume fashion, along with a growing responsibility within the choices we make, this will undoubtedly change future considerations for fashion designers and consumers.

1 Marks and Spencer advertisement in a women's magazine from 1958.

Developing mass-market collections

For corporate branded companies with in-house design teams, the design process is similar to that in high-end fashion. The design team will start developing a new collection whilst still working on the previous one. Elements are often carried across, whether they are successful pieces from a previous collection or core pieces that sell every season. Inspiration boards, or mood boards, will be collated by the design team from their sourcing trips around the world. These boards form an important basis for the design process, reinforcing the design team's vision for the new collection. Information pinned on the mood boards include colour swatches, sketches, photographs, tear sheets, text, illustrations, fabric samples and actual garments, which can be bought for fabric, colour and embroidery references.

Approximately three months before the design process begins, the fabric designers will visit mills to develop specially woven sample cloth known as 'blankets'. Once sketches have been produced and edited, sample garments are made: first in an inferior cloth, such as cotton calico or muslin, and then in the sample cloth. Over the next few weeks silhouettes will be developed; this is an ongoing process where many pieces are discarded in favour of garments that reflect the mood of the season. And so begins the editing process, where approximately 40 per cent of the original sample garments will be shown to the client or on the catwalk. As many as 150 pieces will be made, which represent around 50 looks or exits on to the catwalk or runway.

Once the garments have been shown there will be further adjustments to the collection by the merchandiser, who collaborates with the designer to finalise what to buy and in what quantities for their retail stores. The different ranges are displayed on large, portable grids, each representing drops or deliveries into store; this process is called 'rigging' in the US and 'range building' in the UK. Rigging can represent different colour stories for different labels within the brand. They give buyers, merchandisers and designers an overview of the collection. The editing process should involve distilling and refining looks into tight ranges, which represent the spirit of the overall collection.

1

Ready-to-wear > **Mass market** > Home shopping

Tech packs
Technical packages, or tech packs, are given to factories to produce prototypes for the collections. They usually contain specifications, measurements, fabric, trim and lining information: basically everything needed to produce a garment in the factory.

1   Marks and Spencer womenswear collection S/S09.

2   Banana Republic rigging.

2

1

Designer collaborations

Many retailers have designer ranges as part of their main merchandise. These ranges are manufactured to prices that are more widely affordable than the designers' main collections. In exchange for the designed range and use of the designer's name, the retailer will arrange the sourcing, fabrics, production and visual promotion. This arrangement can be mutually beneficial and profitable for both parties concerned.

The collections are usually designed as 'capsule' ranges, pieces that can be easily put together in whole outfits or looks. Their appeal and success depend on price and creative alignment with the designer's main,

more expensive collection. Some pieces can be cheaper versions of current or past season's pieces. The creative process is exactly the same as if the collection were in a higher market segment, with costs saved in the fabric choices, production volume and profit margin at retail. Many retailers have identified the value and prestige of promoting a guest or celebrity designer to enliven and extend core ranges. This strategy creates opportunities for a new customer group and will also attract the designer's fans. In the US, Target has pioneered this strategy, employing a diverse range of designers to create collections of clothing, homewares and

accessories. Isaac Mizrahi, Todd Oldham and Michael Graves have all helped Target carve a distinctive and design-led profile amongst US retailers. Alexander McQueen is the latest designer to join the Target team, designing exclusive ranges for the brand. Japanese company Uniqlo has also followed this trend by employing Jil Sander as its design consultant.

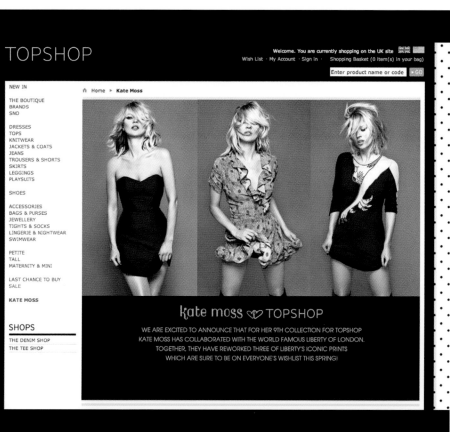

2

Celebrity collaborations

Perhaps the most successful celebrity collaboration of recent times has been the partnership between Sir Philip Green, owner of Topshop, and model Kate Moss. Taking inspiration from her own wardrobe of vintage garments, Kate Moss directs an in-house team of designers. Although not trained or experienced as a designer, Moss has become a living fashion icon and is associated as being the face of a number of brands. Her status and profile is a match for many of the brands and designers who have used her image to promote and define their own products and collections. For Moss to launch a fashion line for Britain's most successful high-street fashion retailer is a shrewd and interesting business development.

1 Ben de Lisi, Betty Jackson, John Rocha and Jasper Conran are just a few of the designers who have collaborated with UK department store Debenhams.

2 The collaboration between Kate Moss and Topshop has been incredibly successful.

Home shopping

1   <www.netaporter.com>

2   <www.asos.com>

3   <www.theoutnet.com>

4   <www.yoox.com>

Originating in 1950s America, the idea of home shopping was to capture the attention of a generation of wives and mothers who stayed at home. One of the original catalogues, Sears, was expansive and covered an enormous range of home and lifestyle products and appliances, as well as fashion. This company and many others became embedded as part of the American way of life; soon after, this form of shopping arrived in Europe and the UK.

The clothing ranges presented in these catalogues were extravagantly illustrated or photographed, often in exotic or aspirational locations and settings. But whilst the clothing ranges were seasonal, they were made in large numbers and stock size and the quality was often average. Garments were designed to be only seen from the front, so the silhouette and backs of garments were basic and dull. This form of fashion production and retail became known as dowdy or downmarket until entrepreneur George Davies launched the Next Directory in 1982. The directory transformed the notion of home shopping. Customers had to pay to receive a copy of the catalogue, which was glossy and featured real fabric swatches alongside photographs and a measuring tape. This interactive experience, coupled with fashion photography by Bruce Weber, featuring models from design magazine campaigns, transformed the idea of home shopping into something cool, informed and exciting. The ranges were clearly influenced by fashion trend and current influential designers. This was the first British retail organisation to understand the concept of 'total look' merchandise and styling. Some items might have been fairly basic, but the overall image and packaging created the desired halo effect for the high-street fashion consumer. For ten years the visual and merchandise format established by Next was influential in endless retail spaces and stores across the UK.

E-tailing

Home shopping today includes online retail, which offers fashion consumers a huge range of merchandise across all brand and price levels.

At the top end of the market is Net-a-porter, which retails pieces from collections brought directly after the designer's catwalk show. Net-a-porter was launched in 1999 and has revolutionised the way women shop. It is successful in its ability to buy quickly from designers and showcase merchandise even

before it is available in some stores. Up to two million women log on a month to browse through 200 leading labels.

Reflecting a younger customer, ASOS has developed an online fashion business which, like a number of other e-tailers, limits availability and produces a large number of ranges across each traditional season. Ranges are designed and produced in a number of countries and stock is carefully planned on prior sales and

time for availability within the traditional buying timescale – autumn/winter becomes available during August and spring/summer comes online in January and February. The original concept was to copy and sell copies of celebrity looks or red-carpet fashion – ASOS is an acronym for 'As Seen on Screen'. The company has since evolved into a successful fashion-centred organisation that strives to produce the latest fashion looks at competitive prices for men and women.

1

2

3

4

Ian Garlant, creative director of Hardy Amies, interview

How do you start the collections?
It's a non-stop process; there isn't a beginning, middle and end. It's one collection that evolves almost directly into the next. We have an autumn/winter collection and a spring/summer collection. The ethos doesn't really change but the colouring, styling and presentation changes all the time. The handwriting and the way we work is fairly seamless.

Would you ever show as part of Couture Week in Paris?
It is unlikely simply because of the cost. There is always a salon show here but there have been occasions where we show outside the House for charities, press and licensees.

Do you still separate between the tailoring and the dressmaking?
It is still separate but there is a crossover and there is now more of a relationship between the workrooms.

Do you collaborate with anyone on shoes and accessories?
We work with Harry Winston for the jewels and for many years it was Cartier and Tiffany & Co. Freddie Fox used to do the hats when Hardy was here, then we went to Philip Treacy on a few occasions. We now work with Stephen Jones for hats and Nicholas Kirkwood for shoes. Jimmy Choo has also done some shoes for our clients so it moves around.

Is your customer getting younger?
Yes, but I think the biggest single change is the increase in professional women who come here for their working wardrobe.

Is it less about evening wear and special occasion dressing?
The two are not mutually exclusive. Some might be corporate entertaining for someone exceedingly glamorous. Professional women need to make a confident, strong presentation of themselves and clothing is of course the ideal way to do that. We have a couple of exceedingly high-powered, professional women who are very low key, the last thing they want is a fuss. What they want is privacy and service as money is not an object. They are very clear about what they want; it's quite anti-fashion.

How many looks are there in one show?
It varies hugely from collection to collection actually. For the Golden Age of Couture at the V&A museum it was over 100. The most recent one was 30-something so it depends on the time and how much we can get done.

Are you fairly sure that what you show will be ordered?
When I put a collection together, I have got a pretty clear idea of what will sell, what might sell and what's used for window dressing or fun, to kick off some other ideas. One case in point this season is a style that we have not sold much of but we have sold a lot of this cloth in other styles. So it's a very good way of maybe demonstrating the cloth.

Do you ever have anyone bringing in a piece from another design house and saying they want something similar?
Yes, but I won't copy another current designer. It is better that they go there and get it. If they have seen a picture of something special or their grandmother has got something, or they have had an idea somewhere, then fine, absolutely. That's a creative process in itself, and I think that is part of the whole discussion in arriving at something you are both happy with. I'm doing a dress for someone that is loosely based on a Madame de Pompadour style. It's an amazing ball gown. She'd seen a picture and said she would like something like that done.

Do you also work with other suppliers, such as specialist embroiderers – the same as the ateliers in Paris?
We work with Hand & Lock in London and we work with embroiderers in India.

How long is the process from the initial meeting until the final garment is delivered?

It can vary vastly from four weeks to a year. If you have got someone who does not live in England and they are only available for fittings when they are here, maybe twice a year, then it will take longer. Quite a number of clients come in from abroad, and what happens after a period of time is that every time they are in England there is something to pick up, something to fit or something to discuss.

Do you keep a stock of fabrics?
Not much as we don't produce that many garments. We are only talking about some hundreds, not thousands, of units. In a season we can produce up to 100 different styles including different colourways and special designs from the original collection. These are normally from merchants who give us short lengths of cloth – usually Parisian, Swiss Italian and Spanish.

Is that difficult for clients who do not want to be dressed the same as somebody else?
Yes, there are one or two occasions, such as Ascot, where I have to be slightly careful. A genuine couture client does not regard the design as necessarily exclusive, but more about having clothes made for their private wardrobe.

1

1   Hardy Amies
     couture A/W07.

Jens Laugesen, fashion designer, interview

What happened after you graduated from the MA?

Lulu Kennedy chose me as one of three graduates to show at Fashion East – part of London Fashion Week. I showed a 25-look collection based on the 16 looks from my graduate collection, which was called Ground Zero. I also designed ranges for Topshop under New Generation.

How do you start your collections?

Instead of every season coming up with new ideas I design trilogies, which are three collections in succession based on the same theme. This way I don't have to come up with new themes for every collection but develop and evolve from the first one. In the 1990s designers were conceptual; now it is the process that is conceptual. I learnt to do this at Central Saint Martins where the method that Louise Wilson uses is to continually break down the process to understand and analyse, in order to rebuild again. As a result of my background in couture, my work is cerebral but wearable, which is important.

How do you research for your collections?

Ideas develop from found objects – mostly garments. I go to flea markets and buy vintage rather than recent clothes.

How many trilogies have you done so far?

I have done 12 so far, starting with Ground Zero from my graduate collection, which was about deconstruction and reconstruction. Then Outsize, which was about analysing the design process; then Future Now to Modernity; and lastly Interior. Here I went back to my Danish roots and studied the work of a Danish artist mixed with glam rock and Paris couture.

How many collections do you design a year?

One main spring/summer collection, one for autumn/winter and sometimes a pre-collection for the US market, as buyers want to buy early and also to see what will be coming out in the main range. About 80 per cent of the orders are placed before the show, with 20 per cent being confirmed from the catwalk three months later.

How do you source your fabrics?

I go to Première Vision and agents come to me. I use fabrics from Italy where they will supply 100 metres; for an extra charge of 30 per cent I can buy short metreage of a special fabric. I also buy from small ateliers in Lyon in France and from wholesalers in the UK such as Whaleys, Pongees and Henry Bertrand. I commissioned a special silk brocade for one collection based on a vintage garment I found. I buy traditional wools for tailoring, then use them in a modern way. I also buy yarn from Loro Piana in Italy for my knitwear ranges.

How do you develop your silhouettes and shapes?

I look at the architecture of the garments and draw line-ups of silhouettes I want to use that season. I research garments by hanging them on a white wall, then I draw directly on to the toiles I have made as replicas of the vintage garments. I sketch only for the pattern cutters and give them technical details. Sensibility in cut and proportion are important and also understanding how the vintage garments were cut by recreating the original. I am interested in turn-of-the-century military garments and Victorian shirts – pieces that are cut for function. Then I mix the elements to create a hybrid – a Victorian shirt with a 1960s dress, maybe; reconstruction from the past in a modern context.

How many cutters do you employ in your studio?

I have two to three cutters working with me every season and then I direct students to work on toiles.

How do you edit your collections?

I look at the final line-up in toiles, then I analyse jacket shapes and trouser lengths for details. I look at the silhouette of that season and photograph each toile from the front, side and back. I have to be objective and then I work with my stylist to edit the final collection.

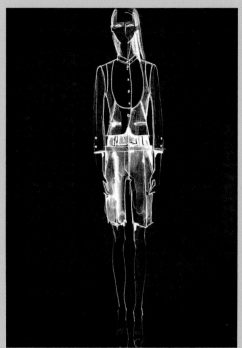

1

1   Illustrations by
Jens Laugesen.

Ohne Titel, fashion label, interview

How do you start your collections?

There's a sense of intuition, then we develop shape and colour. We are designing for intelligent, confident working women who appreciate suitings. We know ourselves what we want to wear and this influences our collection. We also start collecting things that interest us.

How many collections do you design?

Two: fall and spring/summer. We are looking at resort cruise in the future as a collection of easy pieces between the two main collections.

How do you source fabrics and do you compile a colour palette?

We visit Première Vision in Paris, which is inspirational and totally necessary. Reps from yarn mills will also visit us. We have contacts from our previous jobs as designers and are confident in sourcing and putting together colour for the collections. Through discussion and research we will come up with colour chips. We also use the archive at the Fashion Institute of Technology in New York, a library and archive of vintage garments.

How do you develop your shapes and silhouettes?

We drape fabric on the form (mannequin) and use a fit model in the studio. We work directly on toiles and photograph them.

Where do you show your collections?

In a gallery in the West Village on schedule. We subscribe to Fashion Calendar, who set up dates and give us a good position on schedule during New York Fashion Week.

Where do you sell your clothes?

Selfridges and Start, a boutique in Hoxton, London, but not in New York yet. Selfridges will buy 11 of one style and for exclusives, 15–20 styles. Because of selling a small range for the collection we have to look at every piece as being shown on its own.

Who buys your collection?

Madonna has bought our clothes, but we really sell to real women: gallery owners, politicians and business women.

Do you consider sustainability?

Not yet, but we don't use sweat shops. We make in Italy and 90 per cent of our fabrics are from Italy. We also source prints in China but know the factories as quality is important. The French will buy to order and we offer a stock source using colour chips for our prints.

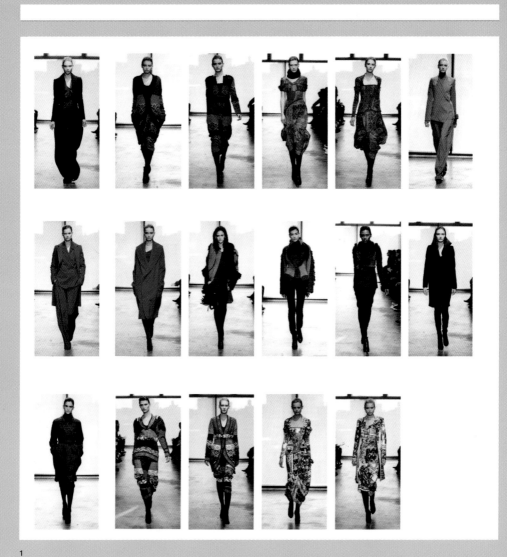

1

1   Ohne Titel A/W08.

Emily Craig, senior designer at DKNY, interview

How do start your collections?

On a big season (such as fall or spring) we start by going to Première Vision in Paris where we begin sourcing the fabrics for the season and getting an idea for mood and colour; at the same time we carry out shop and brand research and do vintage shopping. We have a big vintage/antique library too, with anything from Victorian costume and military uniforms to ethnic embroidery and biker jackets. This is all in-house so it's convenient. There is also a Donna Karan archive housing pieces from each collection dating back to the very first collection in the 1980s. We have meetings with the whole design team to discuss ideas, share thoughts and often we'll have a fitting with a model to try out silhouette ideas and looks.

How many collections do you design?

We design four collections a year: fall, resort, spring and summer. Within each collection, there are three deliveries.

Do you compile a colour palette and if so, how?

Generally our creative director will compile the colour palette but we all discuss it and offer ideas. It can often be based around a great print we've found or from newly sourced fabrics, vintage garments or a photo.

How and where do you source fabrics?

We have a fabric department here, which is responsible for most of the sourcing, but we go to Première Vision as a design team together, or source or develop new fabrics out of Asia and Europe.

Do you commission textiles: knit, print, weave and embroidery?

Yes we do occasionally commission prints and textiles or buy swatches from textile companies, but we also have an in-house graphic designer/textile artist who creates original prints and artworks for us.

How do you develop your shapes and silhouettes?

I tend to sketch mostly but I also work on a mannequin, either draping or working with vintage pieces. We also have an amazing sample room/atelier in-house (now quite a rarity for New York) and I work one-on-one with the pattern cutters to develop the silhouettes and toiles. We also send specs and development to Hong Kong.

Where and how do you create your first samples and how many are made for each collection?

For my styles, as I do tailoring and outerwear, most of the development is done in-house. Some of the soft pieces are made in-house too. This gives us the opportunity to continue developing the collection right up until the line opens. Most of the development of the first samples is done in Hong Kong.

What do you define as a collection or a range?

A concise, coherent collection of pieces that both work together as looks and complement each other.

On average, how many pieces per collection are for catwalk only?

Most of the pieces that make it to runway are adopted on the line for our stores especially in New York, Europe and Asia. Some of the very fashion-pushed pieces are used for press only.

How many looks are in each collection and does this vary by season or line?

For a big season there are approximately 300 styles and 500 single kimbled units, and for the smaller seasons there are about 150 styles and 320 single kimbled units.

How many pattern cutters do you have and how do you communicate your designs to them?

We have two main pattern cutters who work all year round on collection development. I work with one who specialises in tailoring and outerwear and there is another pattern cutter who specialises in soft and feminine pieces. There are also several pattern cutters who work on production patterns; they occasionally help out with development too. I give my pattern cutter a sketch and sometimes an image or a garment along with it to help explain exactly what I want. I will discuss it with him and he will make suggestions or changes. Then he makes a toile or muslin for me to look at and fit.

Do you do in-house reviews of the collections?

Yes, we have 'edit' meetings. This is when we present the collection to the president, executive vice president, merchandising and sales teams. We have these meetings at the beginning of the season when we present the first protos and then with the final protos for line adoption before market opens.

How do you present the collections to your clients?

We have a big showroom where the collection is hung in deliveries along with some looks and accessories, and when the big clients come in we do small presentations with models to show the key looks. At this stage though, the sales team generally takes over. We will have a big 'walk-through' presentation to explain the collection to the sales and marketing teams. This is where we hand over the collection to them and they are responsible, along with the president and executive vice president, for the selling and marketing.

1

1   DKNY womenswear.

Ohne Titel > Emily Craig > James Spreckley

James Spreckley, menswear director at Reiss, interview

How do start your collections?
Emotion-led discussions with the team lead to visual brainstorming sessions. We visit galleries internationally and use sketchbooks. We need to understand the current climate and create a visual mood and create concept boards for colour, fabric and trim.

How many collections do you design?
Four per season for garments in group drops and four per season for accessories. For spring/summer there will be two groups and for autumn/winter the same, with some trans-seasonal drops depending on the season.

How many are in the design team?
Ten in the menswear team covering knit, woven and leather. There are senior designers, junior designers, assistants, product developers and an office manager. Menswear is separate from womenswear but we work on the same floor in a different studio.

Do you compile a colour palette and if so, how?
From the concept mood boards there is a lab dip process using vintage fabrics from garments or images. We only look at trend predictions as confirmation. We will always have a capsule colour collection, which is the core colour palette, and introduce new tones of these. Every season there is exclusive colour development in-house and the lab dips then go out to the factories for sampling. We can have between 45 and 55 variations in tones within colours.

1

How and where do you source fabrics?

We go all over the world to source vintage pieces for development purchasing in New York and Los Angeles. We utilise Première Vision and Moda In, as well as Turkish fairs in London for denim shirting and suitings.

Do you commission textiles: knit, print, weave and embroidery?

We buy vintage textiles and prints for exclusivity in design.

How do you develop your shapes and silhouettes: flat pattern, draping, modelling on the stand?

We model on the stand and flat patterns are produced by our own in-house pattern team.

Where and how do you create your first samples?

We make our first prototypes in-house and through the factories.

What do you define as a collection or a range?

A range is driven by the merchandise but a collection is presented as a creative look. There are ranges within collections, which are updated following sales information and fed back into the collections.

How many looks on average are there in each collection?

For our catwalk shows we have five looks of 30 outfits, so there will be 300 garments in one collection, with about 125 accessory pieces and 20 shoe designs. Seasons do vary, so the size of the collections will vary.

How many pattern cutters do you have and how do you communicate your designs to them?

We have eight pattern cutters who work with the menswear design team. They work from sketches and tear sheets and there is a verbal presentation by the designers. The whole process is hands-on and about communicating information. We also have fittings two days a week on a fit model.

Do you do in-house reviews of the collections?

The design team will have presentations to the store managers who will give feedback and review the collection. We can't change the range once it is done but we can change the way it is promoted through window dressing.

How do you present the collections to your clients?

By presenting to the store managers. They will be given look books and a design pack to 'outfit build' for window displays so that the Reiss identity is maintained. It is important that the outfits are shown how they were designed from the outset. Information is key throughout the business, from mood board to managers who need stories.

Emily Craig > **James Spreckley** > Simon Kneen

1   Reiss menswear A/W08.

Simon Kneen, creative director and executive vice president at Banana Republic, interview

2

1

How do you start your collections?

We start with inspiration from anywhere – exhibitions, vintage pieces that we can rent for a season and shopping in major cities worldwide. We have got to get into it or it is just stuff. The process should be pure and inspirational. We then prepare mood boards; this involves making colour chips from our in-house colour library and from bits of vintage garments or fabric to produce a palette, as well as sketching and creating images from rigging vintage garments.

How many collections do you design all together?

Quarterly, that is, four hits a year – spring, summer, fall and winter, with overlapping elements including previews of menswear and womenswear. The main collections we design by store layout: front, middle and back. The front of the store is high-fashion men's and women's to give an impact of the best of the brand. The middle is city styled, work-appropriate suiting and basic outfitting including the core chino business. The back of the store is weekend chic, calypso styling, holiday, textile and organic ranges. These are brighter and more specialised areas of clothing and accessories, such as swimwear in summer and denim ranges.

Do you collaborate with anyone?

All design is done in-house but we do collaborate closely with our vendors (manufacturers) in the execution of the design. Franchise goods include licensing of perfumes, personal care, sunglasses and jewellery. We also work with Clarks in the UK for men's shoes and Camuto in Brazil for women's shoes.

How many are there in your design team?

There are 62 people in the team of research and developers. Print designers re-colour vintage prints and are creative and imaginative. There is a CAD team and a pre-production team and a mainly British design team.

How do you develop your silhouettes?

We talk through the looks as a group. We use house models for fitting garments. We look at trends in Europe but as the company is bi-coastal we have to be aware of our customer. Banana Republic covers the east and west coasts of America. The GAP headquarters are in San Francisco, where the merchants and buyers are based, and the designers are based in New York. We always filter the brand before designs hit the stores to minimise risks. Our monogrammed collection has a higher price point and can be pushed more. Three per cent of the collection is high risk and only delivered to 30 stores.

Where do you create your samples?

We sample everywhere, all over the world. We produce specifications for new shapes in tech packs.

How important is sustainability and being eco-friendly?

It is not a conscious decision, but one step at a time. Our manufacturers are using fewer chemicals, which has evolved over time. It is a daily routine for them, not a gimmick. Denim washes are ecological through recycling water after stonewashing.

How many stores do you have all together?

There are 400 stores in the USA and 500 globally, so we represent the mass market, each store representing 8,000 square feet of merchandise. We also have an online business for the same merchandise. We have five levels of the total collection – Level 1 for large stores and Level 5 for smaller stores where merchandise is edited according to the store size and location. When we launch a pre-summer range for front of store, the second delivery must flow from it to give a strong fashion message.

1–2 Illustrations by Simon Kneen, as used in the New York and London flagship stores to launch the S/S09 collection.

James Spreckley > **Simon Kneen** > Gordon Richardson

Gordon Richardson, design and product development director at Topman, interview

1

2

How do you start your collections?

For Topman Design it is an in-house team effort. The team works on everything collectively, worked around a theme. The theme is usually a journey through life of a personality at different stages in time. The spring/summer 09 collection was based on two mavericks: Jean Prouvé, an architect who pioneered the use of steel in furniture design; and Graham Obre, who built the first Olympic bike. The team will also look at trends and source vintage clothes from markets such as Pasadena in LA, for styling and proportion.

How many collections do you design?

Two main collections for Topman Design: autumn/winter and spring/summer, which are shown on the catwalk at London Fashion Week. The team will also be designing collections for the Topman range, looking ahead and looking back on sales. They come up with mini trends, which hit the stores at pay weekends. This is a small part of the Topman range, which is displayed at the front of the store and represents a product trend area.

How and where do you source fabrics?

We will source readily available cloth from the stock market in Hong Kong; we may use existing cloth or ends of lines if quantities are small; for example, 100 metres of a fabric.

Do you commission textiles?

If the theme is for chunky knits then a knitwear designer will outsource hand-knits with a company. We have an in-house graphic designer for our prints.

How do you develop your shapes and silhouettes?

We use the vintage finds that the team have sourced and photograph the looks for silhouette and proportion. We mix up shapes: for example, we might exaggerate a shirt to get a strong look under a tailored jacket or have a slim jogging pant and top. The pattern cutter will create new blocks for the silhouettes in the pattern room each season. Our design team communicates on a daily basis with the pattern cutter to develop the pieces.

3

4

Where and how do you create your first samples?

We will send a block, a finished pattern and toile with specifications to our key suppliers in the Far East, who will produce the samples. We usually sample five times what we need for the show.

What do you define as a collection or range?

A collection is an edited, focused point of view and has a 'strong identifiable character'. A range is broader and less specific with wider appeal. A knitwear range for a season will go across many different categories, such as stripes, neck interest or fleece lining. There is a designer each season redesigning and updating the range.

Do you have in-house reviews of the collection?

I will oversee the process from the beginning; Alister Mackie will work closely with me and comes in four times a season. He is the fashion editor of *Another Man* and used to be the senior fashion editor at *Dazed and Confused* so we are confident in his opinion as to how the show should look.

How do you show the collection?

We show as a part of London Fashion Week on the catwalk, which is separate from our MAN show. The MAN show is a showcase of emerging design talent; four designers are selected and sponsored by Topman. We then produce photographs of the show for a static book for wholesale and a look book for the brands.

1–4   Topman menswear S/S09.

Simon Kneen > Gordon Richardson

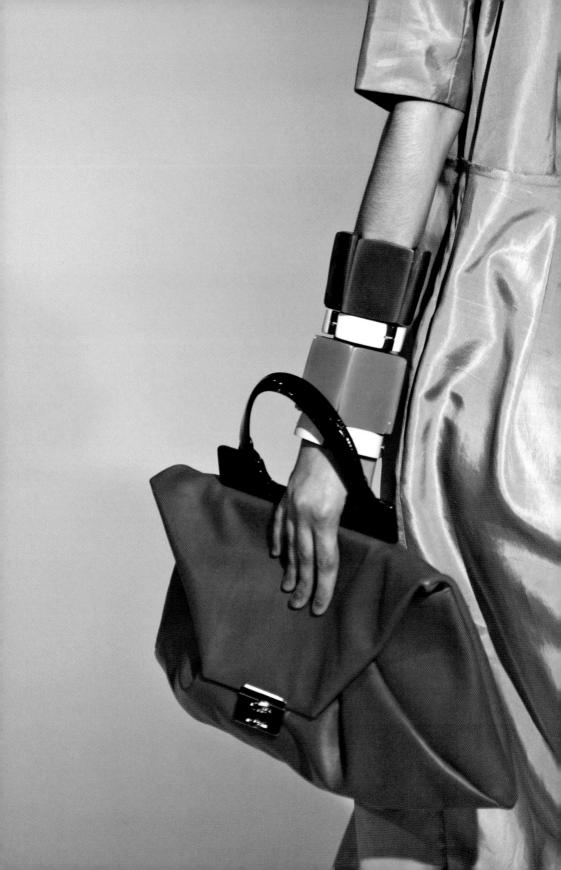

'I would only ask you not to forget to play.'

Alvar Aalto

Collections may be created within specific areas of
fashion, such as children's wear, sportswear, knitwear,
jewellery, footwear and accessories. Most designers and
producers who specialise in specific fashion product areas
ensure that their collections are created and developed to
work with seasonal design trends and directions – or at
least acknowledge and complement them.

Footwear and leather accessories (bags, belts and small
leather goods) can, at times, create strong fashion trends
and influences. These pieces can be used to style the most
basic items of clothing and update a fashion look. Many
established companies rely on sales of footwear, bags,
accessories and licensed lines to maintain their businesses.
Fashion jewellery is also available at all market levels and
has become integral to every fashion occasion and dress
code. Other specialist collections, such as children's wear
and sportswear, are created or commissioned around
specific considerations and situations. This chapter
explores the development of collections within each
of these specialist areas.

Children's wear

1   'Protest is a Mission of
     Passion.' Children's wear
     by Laura Harvey.

Trends within this area of fashion are subtle, but colour, shape
and thematic influences combine to create a niche fashion
movement that often reflects mainstream design in fashion and
beyond. However, a traditional approach persists, and designers
respond accordingly. The design and development processes are
similar to other fashion product areas in terms of fabric, colour and
shape development, sampling and manufacture. Time schedules
mirror the main fashion calendar. As is common in womenswear
and menswear, each designer and retailer has individual sizing
and labelling specifics, which are devised and monitored within
individual businesses.

Many international designers extend their collections from
womenswear or menswear into baby wear and children's wear,
such as Baby Dior, Armani Junior, Moschino Kids and Burberry.
This is an area of the fashion industry that is often overlooked by
students when considering a career, but with most fashion students
concentrating on womenswear or menswear, there are potentially
more job opportunities within this specialist market.

Baby wear

The moment of birth creates a new range of fashion possibilities. Many new parents set about buying clothes that will not only make the child as attractive as possible to friends and family members, but crucially, define the child's sex. It is no accident that pre-birth gifts are carefully gender-neutral in colour and graphics. Lemon, mint and aqua colours are all acceptable for both girls and boys, but the traditional pink and blue base colours will always be a factor in designing baby wear. There are, of course, variations on this depending on geographical region. Italians, for example, will happily dress a newborn boy in garments with pink or coral-coloured trims and details. And the Japanese have, for many years, seen black and khaki as suitable colours for babies and children to wear.

Toddlers

By the time a child is walking, most fashion ranges offer complete looks or wardrobe items including jeans, sweatshirts, shirts and tops, jackets, dresses, trousers and so on. Ranges often reference main fashion trends, including colour, wovens, prints and fabric treatments. Many fashion looks are reinforced through the use of graphics in prints and motifs, as these embellishments can graphically explain the look – often with words, slogans or character names. The ploy is to communicate to the purchaser. This market area is heavily covered with branded or character merchandise featuring popular television, movie or toy characters.

Safety considerations

It should be noted that this specialist fashion market is strictly controlled by health and safety legislation, related to fabric compositions, flammability, toxicity and fastening security. Standards are stringently monitored and particular features of clothing for babies and toddlers are tested. In addition, human ergonomics play a role in the design of the garments. Babies and small children are unable to dress or undress themselves and the logistics of small limbs, sleeves, neck openings and trouser legs must be easy to negotiate. Examination of this type of clothing will illustrate a variety of neck openings and closure details, accommodating the proportional differences between a small child and an adult.

Footwear and accessories

1   Louis Vuitton S/S08.
    Catwalking.com.

2   Bag and shoe design
    development by
    Natalie Frost.

Collections of footwear and accessories, such as leather bags,
can be created as individual fashion statements or may be
commissioned by a designer as a part of a complete fashion look.
It would be impossible to ignore the recent growth and interest
within this fashion area and its influence on consumers' choices.

1

Origins

This specialist area of fashion has a history of tradition, craft, royal patronage and heritage that endures beyond many clothing designers and fashion houses. Medieval craftsmen known as cordwainers made shoes and other articles from fine, soft leather. Cobblers were specifically repairers, not makers. Trade groups were formed to regulate and formalise tradesmen and in 1449, one such group, the Worshipful Company of Girdlers, was granted a Royal Charter to regulate the production of belts and girdles. Other specialist companies were formed around specific leather products, including footwear and gloves. In London, these trade groups represented the highest quality of craftsmanship.

Over time, a number of makers and retailers emerged to establish the origins of the upmarket brands that influence fashion today. Hermès was established in Paris to produce horse harnesses for French noblemen and by 1880, had introduced saddlery. At the same time, the company began its retail business. By 1914, Hermès had secured exclusivity in using the new zip fastener in France for leather goods and clothing. Hermès produced its first bags in 1922. Its most famous bag, created in 1935, was favoured by Grace Kelly, soon to become Princess Grace of Monaco. The Kelly bag is still in production and has a waiting list of 1–3 years.

Global fashion brands Gucci and Louis Vuitton also both started out business in leather. Founded in 1921 in Rome, Gucci began creating and retailing fine leather goods to wealthy patrons. French company Louis Vuitton originally produced high quality travel bags and trunks, which continue in a range of finishes and styles. The company made a strategic shift by appointing Marc Jacobs as creative director. A collaboration with designer Stephen Sprouse in 2001 saw the traditional monogram base fabric being splashed with anarchic lettering and Sprouse's name. This immediately excited the fashion press and a new group of luxury consumers, attracted by this exclusive, high quality (and expensive) range. The company followed this successful collaboration by working with Japanese artist Takashi Murakami to create two distinct interpretations of the monogram line, 'cartoon' and 'cherries'. These, too, were hugely influential and much copied.

Footwear

Many of the processes used in production still rely on handcraft skills and many years' experience to achieve the highest quality standards. Footwear in the middle and mass markets is mostly produced in Brazil, China and Portugal. Footwear made in Italy is more expensive and is therefore found in more upmarket brands. Trainers and sports shoes are mainly produced in Thailand, China and Vietnam, where significant investment has created a profitable, quality-secured industry. Mass-production of footwear has disappeared in the UK, mainly due to labour costs, market changes, and competition from other areas of the world. Footwear is a huge and popular area of the fashion market for consumer and producers. As such, the materials and methods used to create leather accessories and footwear are unique to this product area. Twice each year, Linea Pelle in Bologna showcases trends and developments in leather and leather products. Around 1,300 exhibitors from approximately 45 countries attend this trade exhibition. Exhibitors include tanneries, designers and accessory/component manufacturers. Visiting professionals can find information on related trends and innovations in technology and materials. This is the starting point for many designers. The next stage is to design the fashion shapes for the new collection. A 'last' forms the basis of the shoe, and will dictate the toe shape, heel height and variations on the foot coverage for each style. As for clothing, patterns are cut and then checked against the last. Heels (especially high heels) may be carved or created separately, as these often become embellishments or features of the finished shoes.

Lasts were traditionally carved from wood. At the very top end of the footwear market, companies such as Ferragamo would create personalised lasts for special customers, made to individual specification. Today, rapid prototype technology can create exact requirements for lasts; this is both faster and cheaper than before, thereby adding to the designer's scope for innovation and quick response.

Footwear designers such as Christian Louboutin, Manolo Blahnik, Georgina Goodman and Nicholas Kirkwood create beautiful, desirable shoes. They design special collections in collaboration with fashion designers along with their own ranges. Many of these shoes are produced to the equivalent standards of haute couture clothing: they are expensive, collectable and treasured by consumers across the world.

Specifically aimed at fine shoes for men, Church's Shoes was founded in Northampton in 1873 to produce the highest quality handcrafted shoes for men. The company is still acknowledged as a world leader in this footwear market.

Specialist courses
UK courses in footwear and accessories are offered at London College of Fashion (Cordwainers) and De Montford University, Leicester.

Bags

The bags market is huge and varied. Like fashion clothing, soft leather bags and accessories are created by cutting pattern pieces to be stitched or glued into shape. The colour, finish and leather craft techniques, such as carving, brogue work, burnishing and spraying, can all alter and enhance the surface of many natural skins. Stitching, printing, embroidery and the availability of fixtures, fastenings and strengthening (known as 'furniture' or 'hardware') enable endless design possibilities.

Bags and leather goods are usually developed by an accessories designer or team, and follow the direction set by the fashion clothing – to include colour, silhouette, surface embellishments or treatments. Each item is created in the same way as garments, in that patterns are created and samples are made for approval. Unlike clothing, however, the patterns have to fit the skins; wastage can be high, depending on the type of skin and the size of the pattern pieces, and taking into account any natural flaws and imperfections.

1   Boot designed by Nicholas Kirkwood, A/W08.

2   Shoe design development.

3   Wooden lasts used for shoe-making.

2

3

Knitwear

Yarns
The advanced technology of today's machines means that one-piece, seamless garments can be produced as well as garments in the finest of yarns on fine gauge (which means the number of needles per inch – 16 or 12 for fine gauge). Traditionally yarns were made from natural fibres, such as lambswool, cashmere, cotton, silk and wool. Modern yarns are being continuously developed and improved: synthetic fibres, such as polymide, polyester, microfibre and elastane are all used to create high-performance knitted fabrics.

Machine knitting is produced in one of two ways: flat-bed knitting creates flat fabric, which will be transformed into garments through cut and sew techniques; fully fashioned knitting creates garments that are shaped on the machine. Flat-bed knitting includes the high-end, labour-intensive intarsia knitting, where yarns are laid in the courses of weft knitting to form irregular, one-off patterns and motifs.

Most fashion knitwear is weft-knitted; however, in the 1950s Ottavio and Rosita Missoni in Northern Italy developed colourful patterned artisanal knitwear collections using warp knitting, which is a cross between knitting and weaving. Whilst Missoni reigned in Milan another iconic knitwear designer, Sonia Rykiel was establishing herself in Paris. Rykiel was known as the Queen of Knitwear in the USA and demonstrated 'what you can do with a bit of yarn'. Her collections were based on novelty and slogan sweaters with her signature colourful stripes, classic nautical references and 'boy sweaters'. In the 1970s, Scottish designer Bill Gibb was inspired by traditional craft and ethnic cultures; together with his partner, Kaffe Fassett, he designed some of the most exciting knitwear collections of the decade. Their use of vibrant colours, organic motifs and extravagant layering of knit was influential in the development of fashion knitwear. Gibb went on to collaborate with Missoni, stating at the time, 'What women want to wear in the daytime is beautiful knits'. In the 1990s, Japanese designer Issey Miyake used new technology to create integral warp knitting, launching his iconic 'a-poc' collection, which literally means 'a piece of cloth'. This new concept required the customer to cut up the synthetic knitted cloth, with its computer-generated print, and produce tubular garments that could be worn in a multiple of ways. This innovative process resulted in a capsule collection of a dress, skirt, underwear, hat, gloves, socks and a bag, all cut from one piece of cloth.

Knitwear collections have now come full circle, with designers revisiting traditional handcraft techniques. Designer Clare Tough, for example, combined knit with crochet for her Central Saint Martins graduate collection. At the other end of the scale, London-based designer Louise Goldin creates futuristic body-conscious knitwear that breaks out of all the cosy limitations of sweater dressing. Her complex bodysuits and dresses, created by layering the sheerest of fine yarns, are arguably the future of fashion knitwear.

1   Louise Goldin S/S09.
       Catwalking.com.

2   Missoni A/W08.
       Catwalking.com.

Footwear and accessories > **Knitwear** > Fashion jewellery

Fashion jewellery

Popularised by Chanel in the 1920s, the wearing of fashion jewellery has become a specialist fashion market in its own right. Known as costume jewellery, the pieces worn were obviously imitations of precious or fine jewellery; they were over-scaled and worn as embellishments, rather than formalised signals of wealth or status. Brooches, earrings and rings were worn at social events, weddings and for cocktails, as a finishing accessory to complete an ensemble. Development of new materials in the 1920s, such as Bakelite and lucite, provided new scope for designers to explore different shapes and finishes, whilst defining innovative ways of wearing fashion jewellery.

Good fashion jewellery is a fashion statement in itself; it mirrors mainstream and niche fashion directions, yet lives beyond the seasons, trends and influences that inform the creative processes. Jewellery designers may follow or acknowledge colour and trend information as for fashion clothing.

Scale, surfaces, materials, finishes, fastenings and colour are ongoing considerations for the designer, as are trend developments, such as animal prints, geometrics, fluorescents, high shine and military, ethnic or nostalgic themes; these influences will dictate specific colour and materials. A recurring trend in fashion jewellery takes its cue from global influences, referencing ceremonial jewellery and ethnic pieces.

A number of fashion jewellers are beginning to challenge the definitions of particular types of jewellery and the materials used to create them. Innovative approaches to knitted or crafted fashion jewellery, and the opportunities in dealing with sustainable or renewable materials, are beginning to challenge and redefine existing notions of taste, aesthetics and product. Designers including Marni, Moschino and Marc Jacobs produce seasonal ranges of fashion jewellery to accentuate catwalk presentations and the retail range. Many pieces are created alongside the theme explored within the clothing collection and therefore help to reinforce the narrative or trend being shown.

1   Jewellery collection by
     Giles for Evoke.

2   Marni A/W08.
     Catwalking.com.

2

Corporate collections

Corporate wear is designed to portray a company's image, brand values and in most examples, brand identity. Issues related to health and safety, wearability, durability and care are all factors that inform the final range of garments. Considerations must also allow for the wide range of wearers – body sizing, working environments, religious dress requirements and even personalisation limitations. Colour, prints and logos are aligned to the company's branding in order to promote a unified, professional image.

Banks, hotels, restaurants, retailers and service providers have adopted the approach that employees should represent the company and its mission statement values when dealing with customers. More and more organisations are adding value to the customer experience by employing recognised fashion designers to create corporate fashion collections.

Perhaps the largest corporate investment in fashion, with international recognition, is the uniform worn by national airlines. These garments take years to develop, trial, amend and produce. The range of separates must be suitable for the tasks required of each wearer, whilst conveying professionalism and a dependable authority. Many ranges must also have a fashion lifespan of up to ten years, which presents huge challenges for the designer.

Many airlines are keen to employ internationally recognised designers and as such, the garments have become iconic over the years. Braniff International in the US famously employed Emilio Pucci as part of its entire corporate makeover in the late 1960s. The garments were unlike anything seen before or since; futuristic and colourful, they were as close to fashion as corporate clothing can get. In the 1970s, Braniff commissioned Halston to dress its cabin crews. John Rocha has designed for Virgin Atlantic, Ferré for Korean Air, Balmain for Singapore Airlines, YSL for Qantas, Julien MacDonald for British Airways, Dior and Calvin Klein for Scandinavian Airlines, Armani for Alitalia and Kate Spade for Song. Renowned for the most chic flight attendants, Air France's cabin crews are currently dressed by Christian Lacroix. By aligning themselves with international, premium fashion brands, these airlines are communicating corporate values to customers, as well as adding to the travel experience.

1

BRANIFF INTERNATIONAL

1   Emilio Pucci designed
futuristic airline uniforms
for Braniff in the 1960s.

Mark Eley, of fashion label Eley Kishimoto, interview

How do you start your collections?

On day one we sit down and first ideas are put down in a sketchbook, all drawn from sketches, doodles and illustrations. The beginning of the whole story starts with a word, title or doodle. Research is collated from books, magazines, music listened to, loose notes and from this a little story in a sketchbook becomes an epic.

How many collections do you design?

One main line that is seasonal autumn/winter and spring/summer, including collections of shoes, trainers, bags, small leather goods, jewellery and sunglasses. Also one line for Cacharel.

How you compile a colour palette?

We mix a palette as we go along every season, with Scotdic used by mills for colour reference and buy stock colour fabric as well as greige fabric for dyeing. We mix dyes for prints from the sketchbook. We set the trends and are niche, unlike large corporate companies who rely on colour trend predictions.

How do you source fabrics?

Through Première Vision and agents known for greige fabric to dye. We commission weave and knit lengths from the UK, Italy, Spain, Japan and China.

What do you define as a collection or a range?

A collection is a random grouped amount of things, including catwalk show pieces, whereas a range is a planned number of products. A range plan includes knits and wovens, and covers dresses, trousers, jackets and coats.

How do you develop your shapes and silhouettes: flat pattern, draping or modelling on the stand?

The pattern cutters translate the sketches through a combination of flat pattern and draping. Working from past collections we use various ways of creating finished drawings accurately into garments. We put together the range plan methodically grouped by fabric – a top, skirt, coat, using other colourways and varying weights of fabric. Silhouettes can inspire prints and as all development is in-house we can be flexible. We can also design prints for a particular silhouette.

Where and how do you create your first samples and how many approximately are made for each collection?

We make all samples in-house using three of the best pattern cutters and two sample machinists.

How do you present the collections to the clients?

A fashion show as part of London Fashion week, a showroom in Tokyo, London and Paris and online, which is more accessible to our fans worldwide.

How do you work with stylists and PR for selling the collection?

We don't use stylists as they bring together other people's creative ideas and put them in the magazines. This is our world so we have control of the product and do this all ourselves in-house. PR knows the collection intimately from the first drawing to the final line-up.

1

1–2   Illustrations by Eley Kishimoto.

2

Sibling, men's knitwear label, interview

1

2

How do you start your collections?
We always start with a group brainstorming session, discussing themes or specific ideas that are interesting to us. We do not work to trends or market movements, instead we rely on our own instincts. We discuss images we have collated or found garments we may have gathered.

Are your collections seasonal?
Very much so: as we are knit-specific it is very important to create pieces that are still desirable in summer, which is a challenge. Knit is synonymous with winter and warmth so producing garments that have the correct feel for summer is very specific – yarn selection is key to this.

How do you compile a colour palette?
Colour is part of our initial brainstorming, which will raise questions and ideas for further development and research. This will be readdressed later in the process when the collection has taken form, to ensure cohesion as a range.

1–6   Pieces from Sibling's S/S09 collection.

Where do you source your yarns?
Our yarns are sourced worldwide: Scotland, Italy and the Far East. We have established relationships with many yarn agents, and we visit Pitti Filati, a yarn trade fair in Italy.

How do you develop your shapes and silhouettes?
It is important for us to question traditional shape and form with knit. This has two very contrasting outcomes for us: one is our drive to create new and abstracted forms, challenging what is expected of both a knitwear shape and a menswear form. The other is our joy in creating knitted reproductions of recognised design classics, such as the trench coat, leather motorcycle jacket, boating blazer; feats of engineering that are correct to the smallest detail.

How many are in your team?
Our team has a core of six but this will swell at peak times to about 12. We have people with a great variety of skills: hand knitters, machine knitters, pattern cutters and embroiderers.

Where and how do you create your first samples?
Our studio is a fully functioning knit atelier. We have a wide variety of industrial machinery to allow us to create a great number of our first samples in-house. This allows us to experiment very much more than most companies. We will simultaneously create knit swatches, experimenting with stitch and yarn, and toile the form for fit and proportion. Knit is very different to working in wovens because every garment or design starts with a yarn. We have to build our cloth from scratch for every single piece. This creates both great opportunities and problems.

Where do you show and sell your collections?
We have a showroom in Paris during Menswear Fashion Week, where we invite press and buyers to view the collection. Also we show during London Fashion Week within MAN.

How many looks do you have in your collection?
We try to keep to around 15 pieces. That includes garments that are to appeal specifically to press rather than sales.

Do you work with a stylist and have PR?
We employ a stylist and a groomer for every shoot we produce. It is important for us to consider other professionals' opinions and artistic vision whenever presenting our work. Our PR is all kept in-house. This is vital to us as it allows us to be guarded as to whom we allow to use our product and in what environment. This is necessary to keep our identity clear and consistent.

Do you consider sustainability when producing your collections?
It is a consideration, and we will always go for a more sustainable option given a choice. Ethical treatment of people and manpower is something we are very actively conscious of.

3–4

5–6

Mark Eley > **Sibling** > Katie Greenyer

Katie Greenyer, creative director of Red or Dead, interview

How do you research?

We start off by having a gut feeling on trends that have been cropping up at catwalk shows and looks that key stylists have been pushing. We look at sales figures and see what styles are doing well. We look at trend predictions, such as thefuturelaboratory, but usually our instincts are right. We look at WGSN (fashion and style forecasters) reports to see if there is anything we haven't covered, plus to see what other brands are up to.

We visit galleries and flea markets across the UK and Europe to Russia, China; you name it, if it is key to our trends we will try and get there and experience it for ourselves. We research by going to films, exhibitions, libraries and galleries. We all have cameras and make inspiration boards each week using what we have seen and done. We then publish these boards to all the product teams. We are really our own trend agency. We also have an archive collection of products, sketches, styles, which we revert to quite regularly. We do have a problem storing everything so we tend to photograph it all before it goes off to a warehouse. Our inspiration boards contain fabrics, details and anything that we can chop off and stick on for reference.

How many do you have in your design team?

The Red or Dead design team is small but with all our licensing partners we have become quite big. We all work together, having inspiration days so that everyone is picking up on the same stories and vibes. It's great getting together and having product knowledge from each different category.

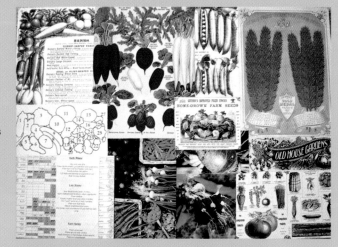

1

2

Where do you produce your samples?
In the Far East, India and Europe.

How do you compile your colour palettes?
From our inspiration and trend boards. We use Pantone references and fabric cuttings for dyeing. We normally produce four inspiration boards: colour, shape, print and graphics.

How do you present the collections?
We will do a presentation of all the range and produce a trend guide for inspiration, colour and packaging for the sales team. We show at Bread & Butter in Barcelona, Basel Watch Fair in Switzerland, Mido in Milan and at Pure London.

How and where do you source your fabrics?
You have to follow the trends and inform the factories what you are looking for, the factories then send swatches to select from. As well as this, the design team visits fabric trade shows and markets for suitable fabrics.

Do you commission textiles, such as knit, print, embroidery or weave?
No, this tends to be done in-house.

How do you develop silhouettes?
We research trends for the coming season looking at the catwalk and look on the high street to pick up on what people are wearing. It's then a matter of creating silhouettes and making them new and fresh and on-trend with a Red or Dead twist.

What do you define as a collection or range?
A collection is a range of garments that covers all product areas so that the consumer can be dressed head to toe in Red or Dead.

How many looks are in each collection?
We work to a phasing calendar that splits the collection up into mini collections. There are usually three to four phases with injection capsule ranges throughout the season to add newness. In each range they will be broken down into casual daywear, core and evening-wear stories.

How many people work on each collection?
This is a mix of designers, product developers and merchandisers, spreading out to buyers and the factories, who all play their own valuable parts.

How many pattern cutters do you have?
None in-house, but the product developers develop specs; they then work with the relevant factories to produce the patterns and garments. Each factory is specialised in specific products and therefore patterns.

Do you have in-house range reviews?
Yes, this is done at prototype stage to ensure that the product is working and is commercial, sits well as a collection and shouts Red or Dead.

Do you work with PR teams?
We work with our PR agency. They work with all our different products and we have regular launches and press days. So they are able to understand our brand and we are able to feed the press samples and stories with just a phone call.

1–2   Red or Dead inspiration boards showing a wide range of research.

Holly Berry, fashion designer, interview

How do you start your collections?

I have several visual bodies of research on the go at one time, consisting of things I've found in the factory, on the street and at markets: photos, archived clothes, artwork and textiles. Whichever body of research is more developed or 'of that time' manifests itself as the foundation of the next collection. To back up this research, before design development I analyse the market, looking at the industry, what our competitors are doing, cultural movements, shifts in style, and popular underground culture.

How many collections do you design?

One full trans-seasonal collection per year, preceded and followed by smaller sample collections and special limited edition pieces to develop looks. I find this a more sustainable approach to fashion and it suits Britain's pretty seasonless weather. This allows me to produce pieces that aren't dictated by fads and trends and acts as a backlash to the current fast-fashion consumer culture.

Do you compile a colour palette?

Other than sporadic injections of colour, I keep colour to a minimum in the collections. Due to the reclaimed content of the product it is best to use black, navy, white and grey, which bring a uniformity to the pieces. Colour is enhanced with vintage prints, tartans and lumberjacks.

1–2   Illustrations by Holly Berry.

How and where do you source fabrics?
From textiles recycling plant LMB and by digging, collecting, picking, cutting and storing.

How do you develop your shapes and silhouettes: flat pattern, draping or modelling on the stand?
Through experimenting (cutting, layering, twisting etc) with classic shapes, inverting them into something instantly recognisable but new.

Where and how do you create your first samples?
In-house by me, the seamstresses and machinists – as many times needed to get it perfect.

What do you define as a collection or a range?
A group of garments all drawn from one source of inspiration to build up a capsule wardrobe of pieces (about 15–20). These can be worn together in many interchanging looks, but each piece must stand equally as strong independently.

On average, how many looks are for catwalk only?
There are two to three show-only pieces: pure unrefined inspiration and unwearable creativity!

How many exits are in each collection?
About 15–20. I design a balanced collection – for example, not all tops or bottoms – then fill in any obvious gaps.

How many pattern cutters do you have and how do you communicate your ideas to them?
One, Kara Messina. We work closely together and use flat technical drawings and rough sketches.

Do you have in-house reviews of the collections?
Yes, at all levels of the business; and also out-of-house with PR press focus groups using Cube PR.

How do you present the collections to your client?
Show, showroom and look book.

Katie Greenyer > **Holly Berry** > Bill Amberg

Bill Amberg, bag designer, interview

How do you start your collections?

I look at the best of the previous year then I look at the merchandise for the entire line and identify roles. Then I chuck it out of the window and start ideas. From my inspiration I pick up a concept, look at detail and also silhouettes established from the previous season. The collection evolves and usually only 20 per cent is new product.

How many collections do you design?

I do two seasonal collections and mid-season drops.

How many are in the design team?

Three, all together. The head of design covers three areas looking after the brand, which is wholesale, corporate and architectural contract business.

Do you compile a colour palette?

Yes, I do mood boards but colours will be influenced by the tanneries, who have their own colour palettes. We also have a few special colour samples done each season.

How and where do you source materials?

We use five different tanneries in the UK and Europe and we develop materials with our favourite suppliers. Leather is the predominant material together with three main fibres: heavy canvas, denim and specialist weaves, such as tweed. We source these from our main suppliers including a webbing supplier.

How do you develop your shapes?

We use four principles when designing bags: silhouette first, which you can see through the window; then the material for feel; then details and finally price. Interior function is a requirement also. For example, men's luggage will need to hold a man's suit or a folded shirt or the length of a shoe. We use flat patterns for shaping, and draping for ergonomic bags, which can be figure-hugging. We have our own workshop in London for sampling new concepts and use our factory for developing samples from existing shapes.

What do you define as a collection or a range?

Each collection has ranges, making a total of six. Each range has three to five pieces and three ranges include small leather goods. Our three main ranges (classics, signature and selvedge) all have a small leather goods range.

How many makers do you have?

Eight people in total in our workshop and we have two seniors and apprentices.

How do you sell your collections?

By appointment in the UK showroom during London Fashion Week. We also show at the accessories fair, Première Classe in Paris and Pitti Filati in Florence.

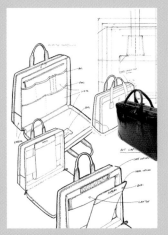

1–3   Designs by Bill Amberg.

1

2

Nicholas Kirkwood, shoe designer, interview

How do you start your collections?
Once production has finished I wait for a gap of two weeks, then I buy a block of paper and with a 2D pencil I draw base ideas continuously for the next collection. My aesthetic is the brand: architectural, feminine, masculine, extreme and always high heels. I divide the 17 or so styles into four sections based on my customers: Leader; Follower; Exquisite and Intellectual.

What is the next process after drawing your designs?
I draw on the vacuum form prototype last to make the first pattern (instead of on masking tape on lasts, which is the traditional way). I then hand this over to a *modeliste* (pattern maker) in Italy. My shoes are high-end and handcrafted rather than computer generated.

Do you look at the work of other shoe designers at all?
Only to check that I am not doing the same designs. My new designs are usually a new interpretation on a few styles.

How many collections do you do in a year?
Two main collections: one for spring/summer and one for autumn/winter. I show in my studio during London Fashion Week in September and February and I also show in Paris, Milan and New York. Micam, a trade show in Milan, overlaps and I invite press to a hotel there.

How many are in your design team?
Just me! Christopher, who works with me, covers sales, marketing, production and suppliers. He will range plan and merchandise each group and is responsible for the 29 or so samples I will produce in different fabrications within the 17 styles in the collection.

Do you produce a colour palette for each season?
I go to the leather fair at Linea Pelle in Bologna at the end of October and see ranges of coloured leather. It is important to have colour balance in the range; for example, last season I did black shoes with electric blue heels. I will usually choose four or five colours that sit well together. I can also dye small quantities for special colours.

How and where do you source your skins?
I use mainly leather and suede and I also use satin, which is stiffened with backing cloth especially for shoes, all from Italy. Vintage shoes are often in kidskin but I don't use it for collections as I like to use new-looking leathers and special skins such as alligator.

Do you commission embroidery or other surface decoration?
I have worked with Swarovski to soften the hard architectural, angular lines and this application will add delicacy to the shoe.

How do you work on your shapes?
Once I have the initial paper pattern from my drawing I will refine and change it by maybe adding pleats or adding a platform heel. I can get a shoe sample made in two days from a new last shape and heel shape. For a new heel I have an aluminium mould made in two sizes: 35 and 41. For production there will be four sizes of heels: 36, 37.5, 39 and 40.5. The samples are one-offs and my shoes have hidden parts to hold the foot, disguised by a more extravagant outer part – similar in construction to architecture. Shapes are usually in stories of two.

Do you collaborate with other designers or companies?
I design shoes for Pellini, who also has Jonathan Saunders as a designer, and Alberta Ferretti in Italy as well as my main line. I have also made shoes for Hardy Amies, Chloe, Boudicca, Gareth Pugh, Clare Tough, Basso & Brooke and Zac Posen.

Do you have a PR company working for you?
Yes, I use Relative PR, who also represent Christopher Kane in London.

1

1   Nicholas Kirkwood cross
hash sandal A/W08.

1   London College of Fashion
RA show; a pastel
chiffon/Lycra collection
by Fiona Broni.

'One desire that is getting stronger than all other demands remains the desire to be unique.'

John Galliano

Studying on a fashion-based course offers you time to develop your imagination, improve your professional awareness and respond to a series of challenges.

Initial projects will focus on learning and applying creative, practical and contextual skills within defined fashion project briefs. These briefs may include designing and producing two- and three-dimensional ideas as an individual or within a team. For instance, you may have had to respond to the parameters within a brand, season, customer, fabric type or story, or perhaps had to consider additional factors such as working with print or knit specialists as part of your study.

As a guide to the processes involved in the creation and realisation of your final collection, the following activities represent the key stages of process. Be prepared to keep a cross-check between each stage, as you may need to go back to revisit an element of research or early development when reviewing your progress and considering the final presentation. There are no clear end points to each stage; even at the final presentation there are elements that could be redeveloped or refined. This is symptomatic of fashion where creativity is not just about problem solving but producing a proposal or statement that should intrigue or connect with the onlooker. The most successful student collections tell a story; they embody a captivating narrative. The collection must communicate this without the visual research or written explanation. This chapter will help guide you as you develop your own, final, student collection.

The brief

1 Garment development by Laura Thompson.

2 'On Being an Angel' by Francesca Sloan. Collection based on photographer Francesca Woodman contrasting with the musician Patti Smith.

This may be referred to as the final brief, proposal, statement of intent or concept outline. Regardless of its name, the activity and process is the same. Begin by asking yourself what will showcase your skills and creativity in the best way. Some students approach this stage of their final collection with vague or unrealistic ideas, being driven to making the ultimate, personal catwalk statement. Without reflection, research and a great deal of hard work, this will not work. Creativity in fashion exists within a context – and for this final college collection, you create your own context, within your brief. On the following pages, we will discuss the considerations that should inform your brief and collection.

1

Your skills

You should think hard about your particular strengths. For example, are your skills in cutting and garment making? Do you have a good use of colour? Perhaps you have proven abilities in collating research materials to produce a confident, well-rounded conclusion. Most employers are looking for graduates who can demonstrate an understanding of the stages of design through to realisation. The presentation of your collection is important, but your portfolio, personal presentation and depth of understanding will secure your first and subsequent jobs. Decide what this collection will say about your interests and your awareness of fashion.

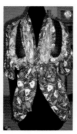
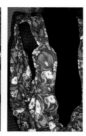

The brief > Your portfolio

Your customer

Consider defining your ideal customer. By imagining a customer you can begin to create your own muse or inspiration. Where does your customer live and what is in his or her wardrobe? Where do your customers shop and how do they wear fashion to define themselves? Go and visit the shops you would identify as stockists for your collection, and look at the existing stock. Detail the prices and the finish on the garments and begin to inform yourself of the realities of market levels, visual merchandising and how fashion communicates through branding and creative identity. How do clothes connect with customers at the point of retail? When we buy fashion, what stories do we tell about ourselves?

1

Your competitors

Your competitors exist in every fashion area, market level and retail possibility. Your work may be innovative, or redefine a particular area, technique or product, but fashion is a discipline that exists in a wider context and constantly references itself – past and present. Even if you approach fashion as art rather than design, you will be able to find a range of practitioners and collaborators who have taken this view. Once you have a clear idea of your product and market type then you should be able to identify the competition.

Quality, luxury and rarity can be defined in any product, so once you know who your competitors are, study their products closely. There is no substitute for trying clothes on and seeing first-hand how the garment feels, examining the cut and stitching. Look too, at details such as buttons and the quality of any branding or labelling. At the other end of the scale, you should be prepared to look at mass-market fashion as ranges are often on-trend and produced to appeal to greater numbers of fashion consumers.

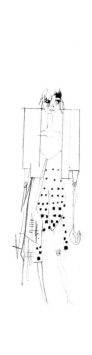

2

Remember, too, that your fellow graduates are your competitors. You could consider niche areas such as plus-size fashion, swimwear, children's wear and evening wear, for example, which will provide you with a specific starting point. These can help position you for the future as you will stand out from the hundreds of womenswear-related graduates who enter the jobs market each year, and increase your potential in securing employment. Most employers look for evidence of research, development, realisation and presentation within a portfolio.

These skills are easily showcased by collating your portfolio as a series of projects, to show diversity and competence across different ranges, market-based studies and self-defined work – which is typically your final college project.

1   Sketch by Michela Carraro, inspired by black lilies.

2   Illustration by Felicity Haf.

Achieving your aspiration

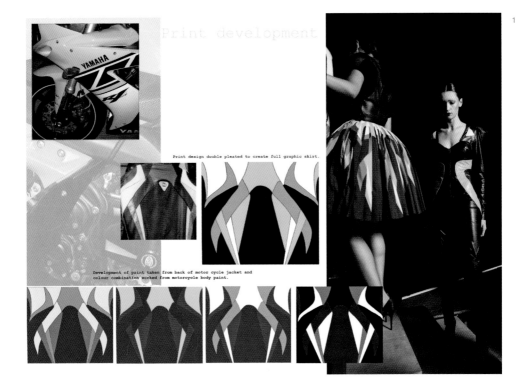

Print development

Print design double pleated to create full graphic skirt.

Development of print taken from back of motor cycle jacket and colour combination worked from motorcycle body paint.

1

If you realise that you will need assistance and input to produce your collection, you have the opportunity to build a team to make this happen – as most designers do. Time planning, delegation and management of the project are part of the whole process. A good starting point is to have a draft collection plan (or line-up) where you can begin to deconstruct each piece into activities and deadlines. Use a calendar to plot key dates against the processes involved – this will help you to get organised and manage your schedule. Allow enough lead time to secure sponsorship for fabrics, trims, shoes and so on. Remember also that most students will be thinking, writing and developing ideas at the same time as you.

1   Design development by Holly Brown.

2   Fabric design development by Emma Glynn.

2

Cost

You should be realistic when planning and costing your collection. Fabrics, finish and trims should reflect a realism within your chosen market or your target customer. Again, pay close attention to how clothes are cut and finished. If you are aiming for an upmarket collection, the typical retail price may be up to 300 per cent of the wholesale price. If you have made any industry contacts as part of your study (work placements, sponsored projects or visiting speakers from industry), then you should consider contacts as potential support or sponsors. Some student collections can cost huge amounts of money to produce, but this is not a prerequisite for success.

Fabrics, yarns and trims

Buying fabrics in retail outlets should be your last resort. Visit trade fairs such as Première Vision for fabrics, Pitti Filati for yarn and Linea Pelle for leather. These shows provide a wealth of contacts and agents for sourcing fabrics, trims and specialist details. Whilst most manufacturers are initially unwilling to deal with students – due to the small quantities being ordered – it is possible to buy from stock sampling if the minimum order is agreeable. Agents may also hold some sample stock that needs to be cleared at the end of the buying season. The Première Vision directory contains valuable information on manufacturers, contact details, fabric types and so on. You should also consider visiting mills and any local suppliers, as these sources often provide high-quality fabrics at lower costs.

Market level

All fashion has a market level, regardless of the type or occasion. If you feel you have no competitors or that no one else is making a similar product (in terms of cost or type), then you need to research further. Although aesthetics and creativity are defined by each designer or manufacturer, a visit to a high-quality department store, in the concessions or designer area, will show you how market-level definitions are made and stocked at the business end of fashion.

Your portfolio

Your portfolio should include:

- Illustrations
- Technical drawings (flats)
- Sample board of fabric, trims and finishes
- Initial research boards
- Photographs of final garments, either from a photoshoot or catwalk show
- Final look book of collection
- Press cuttings, CVs and business cards

Your portfolio will ultimately secure your first job or a place on a postgraduate course. Within your portfolio, you should show the process and outcome of your final collection – through edited research and development, images and photographs of the final outfits. If you have shown your collection in a static or catwalk show, include good-quality images from the event to showcase your work as professionally as possible.

A comprehensive portfolio will contain at least six projects covering a range of activities and different types of design work. Be sure to include examples of colour development, IT applications, technical drawings, range plans, any industry-linked work, use of textiles and so on. Most professional portfolios feature a list of contents and page breaks to section off each project. If you wish to produce a digital portfolio, remember that anyone looking at this will not be able to touch fabrics or trims as part of the viewing (which is also true of plastic sleeves). Keep your portfolio clean, ensure that it is manageable and easily portable and be prepared to update it or reconfigure it, depending on the type of interview.

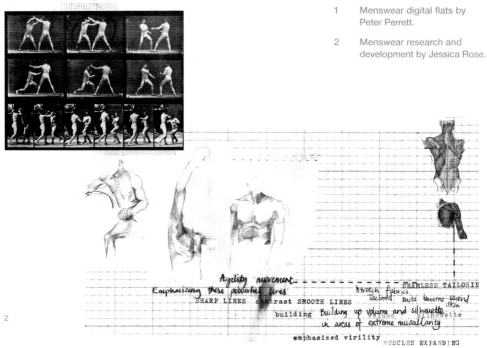

1 Menswear digital flats by Peter Perrett.

2 Menswear research and development by Jessica Rose.

Research materials

It is commonplace to include evidence of source materials and all research activities, which will constitute the main part of your portfolio. This provides evidence of your skills related to research, development and presentation of materials. A sound portfolio should contain a minimum of five to six projects to encompass variety, product differences, colour, print, silhouette, occasion and so on. It is important to show a design identity, as well as creative diversity. Be rigorous and present an edited, considered representation of the whole process. Too little work will look scant and poorly informed. Too much will look confused and busy.

Look at how magazines lay out images and text. Study books on related design subjects such as graphic or textile design, architecture, furniture and product design. Upmarket catalogues or leaflets from cosmetic, electronic and car manufacturers are often beautifully produced with huge financial budgets. Study these and deconstruct how and why they look so effective and beautiful. Once you can identify this process and methodology to powerful two-dimensional imagery, you can transfer this thinking to your own work with powerful, confident results.

Drawing

Drawing is a fundamental process in visual communication, from initial quick reference sketches to fully rendered illustrations. Most fashion courses look for evidence of drawing in interview portfolios.

However, drawing has become a much wider descriptor in the fashion industry, which requires technical drawing, range planning and specification documents. The development of various software packages has enabled fashion students to replicate a number of industry standard processes and techniques when presenting fashion ideas and collections.

The brief > **Your portfolio** > Research and development

Research and development

1 'The ragpicker recycles the ruins of modernity' – menswear research by Kasha Crampton.

2 A double-lace shoe designed by Kasha Crampton in collaboration with JJ Hudson of Noki.

3 Design development drawings by Emma Glynn.

Research will form the basis for your collection and you will need to gather an exhaustive range of source materials. These will include specific investigations into fabrics, colour, silhouette shapes and details as well as live events and imagery in the form of drawings and photographs – in fact, a broad coverage of everything that will inform and influence your thinking and decision making. As you go on to develop your collection, which involves editing, refining and amending your initial proposals, it is important that you have enough research to allow for this. The visual presentation and collation of this body of work should illustrate the breadth and detail of your thinking in an exciting and dynamic way. This is vital, as you will revisit this stage of the project as you progress towards the later stages. Visual materials should speak for themselves and illustrate your thinking and development.

1

'The rag picker recycles the ruins of modernity. He or she is an urban archaeologist who unearths the old-fashioned commodities that in turn reveal the truth about new ones.' _Walter Benjamin.

2

Sourcing

Try to avoid downloading simplistic images from websites or using too many tear-sheets from popular magazines, as this usually equates to a perception that you could have done more work elsewhere. There is no substitute for discovery and innovation through primary research.

Consider compiling your research into various categories – inspiration, colour, fabrics, shapes and accessories. You may find it useful to write a short story or narrative that explains your process or defines the overall approach. Try creating characters or situations from history, fantasy or everyday life to provide a

basis for your research. You may be inspired by a book or a film. If so, investigate more about the author, theory or context by looking at other related examples. Keep a small notebook with you for notes and sketches. Take the time to go to vintage shops and markets, or even auction websites such as eBay, as these are a valuable source of original garments to dissect and rework. Museums or galleries also offer the best initial contact with inspirational materials. Write letters or emails for appointments to discuss your project with the experts or connections to the materials you need. If you are interested in using

colour to make your collection memorable, research established colourists in fashion and textiles and consider what you could learn from their successes. Great designers are fastidious on research and detail, with collections referenced in full.

The more preparation and investigation put into this stage, the better prepared you will be when you have to make subsequent decisions or undertake more specific research and sourcing.

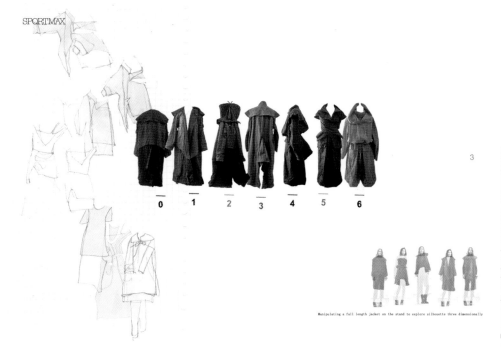

SPORTMAX

0   1   2   3   4   5   6

3

Manipulating a full length jacket on the stand to explore silhouette three dimensionally

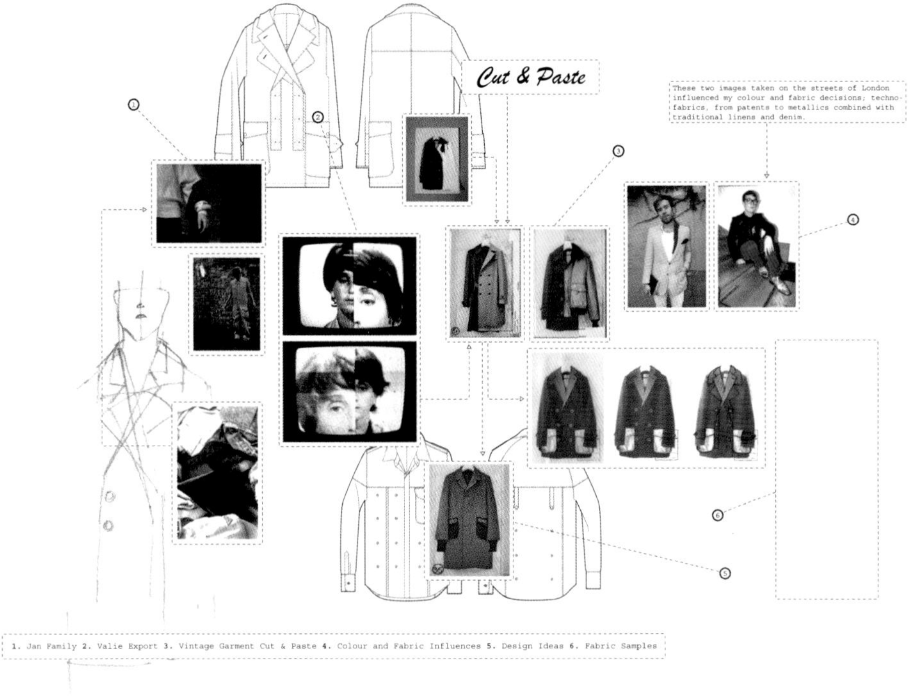

Cut & Paste

These two images taken on the streets of London influenced my colour and fabric decisions; techno-fabrics, from patents to metallics combined with traditional linens and denim.

1. Jan Family 2. Valie Export 3. Vintage Garment Cut & Paste 4. Colour and Fabric Influences 5. Design Ideas 6. Fabric Samples

1

Designing from your research

This stage of the process, known as design development, bridges your research into the final outcome. As such, this stage will involve working with the key aspects of your research – images, drawings, fabrics and so on – and interpreting them in your designs. Drawing together each detail, it is possible through thought and reflection to assemble a series of visual collages that will contain your preferences and ideas allocated to each piece and outfit.

It is important to remain flexible and open to change as ideas may not work as initially thought, or availability of fabrics may change. Use drawings and photographs as an easy visual resource to explore ideas and permutations.

Outfit 5

Wool Coat with detatchable colapsable
hood, Trouser hook Front fastening and
Technical silk scarf- Military Cotton straight
leg Trouser- Washed Leather collapsable
Breifcase.

2

Realisation

At this stage, you will be moving
into the realisation of your ideas –
through pattern making and toiling,
draping and constructing the first
samples. You may also be printing
and knitting samples that will be
used as a part of the final
presentation of your collection. By
this stage you should be sourcing
and organising your trims, ordering
fabrics and perhaps working with
additional producers – knitters,
printers, accessory designers
and jewellers.

1   Research and technical
     drawings by Alex James.

2   Final collection by
     Kasha Crampton.

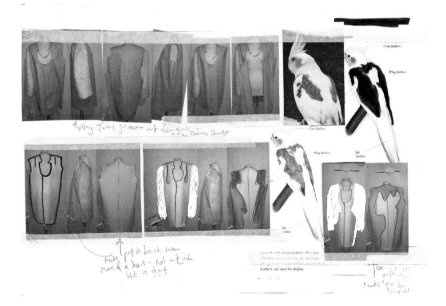

3

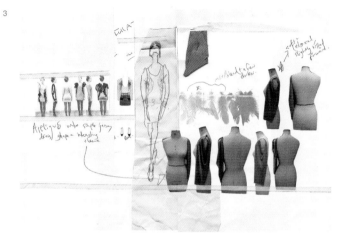

1–5 Design process through
toile and line-up review by
Rebecca Carpenter.

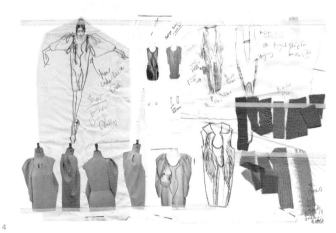

4

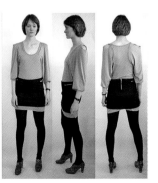

5

Project managing

Consider drawing up a production chart or critical path for each piece of your collection. This will help you manage your time and to make decisions when problems occur. It is always a good idea to have an initial line-up or range plan so you can remind yourself of tasks completed and those areas that are more time-hungry. You need to see the whole project coming together against time constraints, critical deadlines and input from your tutors. You should be prepared for disasters and aspects that don't go to plan, such as fabrics that are out of stock or toiles that don't work. Perhaps some work takes longer than planned, or there may be hidden costs and promises that fail to materialise. These are difficulties that designers and producers encounter all the time and, although difficult, these challenges can be overcome whilst preserving your vision and planning. Try to remain flexible and positive throughout.

Documenting and preserving research

Be prepared and photograph your toiles, fittings and stand work. Photographs will provide you with a clear record of your development and any refinements needed as part of this process. You can also plan for a review or critique with tutors or other students by using your photographs as part of your range plan or collection line-up.

Remember to keep records of fabrics, trims and anything related to each garment. The photographs and drawings will illustrate only part of the story and it is difficult to envisage some toiles in the finished (or proposed) fabric.

Your drawings, swatches, samples and prototypes should convey a clear message, but they may be experimental and can always be rethought or discussed. Your two-dimensional work and three-dimensional development should be allowed to evolve; don't resist drawing on a toile or photograph to keep your imagination stimulated and your judgement sharp.

Reviewing

Ensure that you are prepared and ready to present your work at review points. This is an opportunity to discuss your work and should be challenging yet constructive. Whilst it is important and helpful to be able to present your research visually and verbally, the story being told should ideally work without the need for verbal explanation. Any tutorials or reviews will, of course, involve conversation, advice and an exchange of viewpoints, but if you find yourself explaining your research at length then perhaps you do not have enough visual research, or it may be muddled. The final portfolio and collection presentation will not be accompanied by a verbal narrative and it will succeed or fail on its ability to communicate to the audience. Remember, you are telling a story through images and finished outcomes. Images, drawings, fabrics and activities should be carefully placed and related to specifics so don't, for example, show an image and then the final collection. Taking time to prepare at this stage is invaluable and will help you get the most from presenting and discussing your work.

Make yourself aware of what is expected, who will be part of this review, and what you hope to gain from it. If you have questions relating to your work, write them down and if the points are not covered as part of the review, ask for a few moments at the end. Successful reviews are based on a dialogue, so although you may feel nervous (or worried if you know you are behind schedule), know that, for your progression, your tutors want to work with you to arrive at the best possible outcome.

Throughout the review process, editing will be expected: for example, an idea may be better developed within another garment or outfit, or you may have to select from looks that are becoming repetitive. At this point, the rejected elements will have to be replaced, based on the development of the rest of the collection. This process is evolutionary and it reflects professional practice. It is almost impossible to plan and systemise the entire process without revising and reworking ideas.

2

1   Rough planner for collection.

2   Final collection by Rachel Buck.

Presentation

Your final submission or presentation will comprise of the final collection, a look book and all source, research and development materials. The final collection in three dimensions will be specified to your course requirements, but will usually be displayed on a rail and arranged in complete outfits or looks. You may also have to include patterns, toiles, specification sheets or costings and technical files to support the collection and evidence the process from start to finish. Different fashion-based courses have specific requirements that reflect the curriculum content or specialisation.

Designer collections can be anything upwards of 15 looks or outfits. An undergraduate student will typically produce a prototype collection of six outfits as a part of a college show. Postgraduate fashion students may produce 12–15 outfits. These typical figures reflect the scheduled student timetables and the students' skills and level of experience. In addition, whereas most designers' shows run for a maximum of 20–25 minutes, undergraduate fashion shows will run for no more than 45–50 minutes, so six outfits is generally acknowledged as an adequate number of outfits for each student to convey the theme and content of the collection (and also allows enough time for the show to feature the selected students).

Graduate fashion shows

Most student shows will have a running order of 20–30 students (known as exits in designer shows), although many fashion-based courses are much larger.

A selection process takes place in nearly all fashion colleges for a press or event-based show (such as Graduate Fashion Week in London) and each college will have its own criteria for selecting the final show order. Often a panel of judges is convened to view the range of collections that will make for the best show possible. Judges will be looking for cohesive, well-cut and well-finished clothes that will contain enough visual narrative to tell a story or communicate to the audience.

There is no formula for certainty in this selection. If a number of students have, for example, produced a range of black jersey womenswear separates it is unlikely that, given choice, all collections will make the final running order. No college wants to show a lack of creative diversity and run the risk of an unhappy audience or negative press coverage. Likewise, it is unlikely that a complete show will be entirely made up of hugely dramatic, theatrical clothes, as this is unrepresentative of fashion as a whole. Beautifully crafted, effortless clothes are irresistible and make for a great show – even if they are not entirely for everyday wear.

Study web-based media to read show reviews and where possible look at college websites and DVDs to see examples of choice and show presentation. Remember, however, that although a show can be a great profile builder, or press focus, your portfolio is arguably as important for your future.

① ② ③ ④ ⑤ ⑥ ⑦

Research and development > **Presentation**

1

The look book

The look book or visual line-up will show each of the outfits on models, or arranged to convey the intended fashion story. A look book is a photographic range plan produced by designers, manufacturers and retailers each season or for each fashion story. Sometimes the fashion looks are photographed from a catwalk show or as individual pieces – such as accessories and footwear. The books are designed to assist buyers to make their choices and to merchandise across their buying budget. Retailers use look books to recreate in-store merchandise stories

and as visual aids for windows or displays. Your version is intended to convey your complete fashion look or story. Styled photographs work well, but however you illustrate your work, it should be clear and informative and link together. Try not to over-decorate. The images should convey the complete design process leading up to the final outcome.

1   Final collection line-up by Bahar Alipour.

2   Final collection by Sharnita Nandwana.

2

Styling

You should consider the styling and total look possible within any fashion range. Whilst it is easy to design footwear, accessories and jewellery on paper, it is fairly straightforward to customise inexpensive or thrift shop finds. These additional pieces can be key to the overall design statement – at times they can propel a range of garments into an innovative fashion statement through humour, drama, colour or whimsy. This consideration also confirms your attention to detail and ability to direct a complete fashion statement.

When planning and constructing a styling shoot, you should research and plan for the overall look you are trying to achieve. A good starting point is to gather a selection of high-quality magazines aimed at a variety of readers. *ID, Paper, Vogue Italia,* and *Pop* are just a few examples of magazines that feature the industry's best photographers, make-up artists and stylists. Each photographic image has been painstakingly constructed, styled, lit and photographed. The best styling images convey a clear, powerful

message. In fashion, this usually emphasises an aspect of the clothes being photographed (such as silhouette, proportion, scale, volume, colour and so on), or a dynamic contrast where hugely expensive garments are featured in unusual settings. Having begun to understand how styled images are configured, you are better prepared to create your own.

Aesthetic
A set of principles underlying the work of a particular designer or artist. In fashion design, this means the way in which a designer uses fabric, cut, scale, colour, texture and references.

Atelier
A workshop or studio used by an artist, designer or a couturier.

Comp shop
The comparison of competitors' stock in terms of fabric, construction, detailing, price and manufacture.

Costing
The estimated cost of producing a garment.

Drops
The introduction of collections or ranges in mass-market fashion stores. Drops are often staggered throughout the season.

Exit
A complete look as worn by a model on the catwalk or runway.

Flats
Technical drawings showing garments front and back, usually forming part of a 'tech pack'.

Forecasting
The process of predicting forthcoming fashion trends.

High-street fashion
UK term for mass-market fashion.

Last
The rough form of a foot, used as the basis for making shoes. The last determines the size, shape and style of the shoe.

Line-up
The edited collection for catwalk or look book.

Look book
Used for press, buyers and customers, a look book shows the collection styled and photographed into 'looks'.

Mood board
Compilation of research materials, images, colours, fabrics, sketches, grouped together to visually communicate a theme or design idea. Also known as inspiration boards.

Muse
A person, usually a woman, who is the source of inspiration for a designer or artist. Often, a designer's muse will have creative input in the design process – for example Lady Amanda Harlech, who works with Karl Lagerfeld at Chanel.

Off-schedule
Designers, often contemporary and up-and-coming, who show alongside the scheduled shows during a particular fashion week.

Palette
A group of colours that sit well together.

Prêt-à-porter
French term that literally means 'ready-to-wear'.

Rigging
A US retail and design term, refers to a collection or range in-store.

Sample
The first version of a garment made in the main fabric.

Silhouette
The outline shape of a garment or collection.

Stock-keeping unit
A way of tracking sales, allowing a merchandiser to analyse the way past-season garments sell.

Tear sheet
A page cut or torn from a publication, often used on mood boards.

Tech pack
Technical package supplied to a manufacturer, containing costings and detailed specification sheets of sketches, flats, measurements, fabric and trim references and special instructions or finishes.

Toile
The fabric sample used for fitting a garment, usually made in calico or inferior fabric.

Vertical production
Refers to the way in which a retailer produces garments; a vertical producer, such as Zara, controls every aspect of the design and manufacture process.

BE PURE
BE VIGILANT
BEHAVE

Banana Republic
www.bananarepublic.gap.com

Bill Amberg
www.billamberg.com

Brooks Brothers
www.brooksbrothers.com

DKNY
www.dkny.com

Eley Kishimoto
www.eleykishimoto.com

Hardy Amies
www.hardyamies.com

Jens Laugesen
www.jenslaugesen.com

John Varvatos
www.johnvarvatos.com

Kenneth Mackenzie
www.sixeightsevensix.com

Markus Lupfer
www.markuslupfer.com

Nicholas Kirkwood
www.nicholaskirkwood.com

Ohne Titel
www.ohnetitel.com

Red or Dead
www.redordead.com

Reiss
www.reiss.co.uk

Richard Nicoll
www.richardnicoll.com

Shelley Fox
www.shelleyfox.com

Sophie Hulme
www.sophiehulme.com

Topman
www.topman.com

Vivienne Westwood
www.viviennewestwood.com

William Tempest
www.williamtempest.com

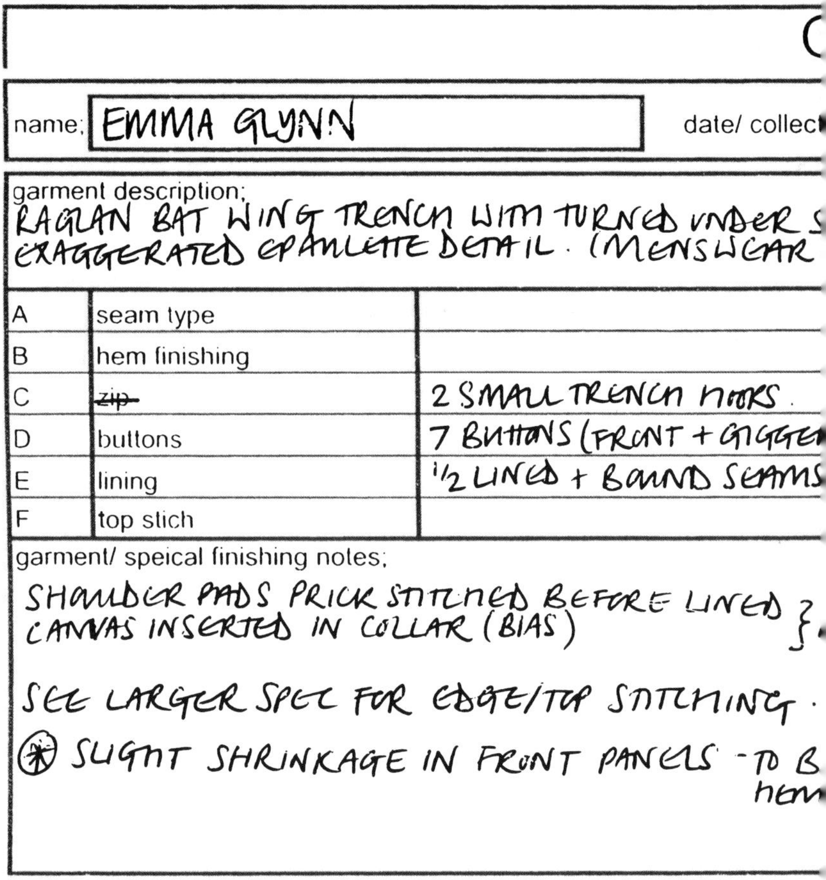

name: EMMA GLYNN   date/ collect

garment description:
RAGLAN BAT WING TRENCH WITH TURNED UNDER S
EXAGGERATED EPAULETTE DETAIL. (MENSWEAR

A	seam type	
B	hem finishing	
C	~~zip~~	2 SMALL TRENCH HOOKS.
D	buttons	7 BUTTONS (FRONT + EXAGGER
E	lining	½ LINED + BOUND SEAMS
F	top stich	

garment/ speical finishing notes:
SHOULDER PADS PRICK STITCHED BEFORE LINED }
CANVAS INSERTED IN COLLAR (BIAS)

SEE LARGER SPEC FOR EDGE/TOP STITCHING.
(✳) SLIGHT SHRINKAGE IN FRONT PANELS - TO B
hem

SHOPS AND SUPPLIERS

Blackout II
(Vintage clothing and accessories)
51 Endell Street
London WC2H 9AJ
www.blackout2.com

Borovicks
(Fabrics)
16 Berwick St
London W1F 0HP
www.borovickfabricsltd.co.uk

Creative Beadcraft
(Beads and sequins)
20 Beak St
London W1F 9RE
www.creativebeadcraft.co.uk

John Lewis
(Fabrics and haberdashery)
Oxford Street
London W1
www.johnlewis.com

MacCulloch and Wallis
(Fabrics, linings and haberdashery)
25–26 Dering St
London W1S 1AT
www.macculloch-wallis.co.uk

The Bead Shop
(Beads)
21a Tower Street
London WC2H 9NS
www.beadshop.co.uk

The Button Queen
(Buttons)
76 Marylebone Lane
London W1U 2PR
www.thebuttonqueen.co.uk

The Cloth House
(Fabrics)
Berwick St, London
www.clothhouse.com

The Observatory
(Vintage clothing and accessories)
20 Greenwich Church St
London SE10
www.theobservatory.co.uk

What the Butler Wore
(Vintage clothing and accessories)
131 Lower Marsh
London SE1
www.whatthebutlerwore.co.uk

Developing a Collection

ment spec sheet

garment: TRENCH

working drawing; front & back

HANGING LOOP - SELF.

EPAULETTES
= EDGE
STITCHED

PRICK/
STAB STITCHED

JER +
VING)

MALLER (BACK
VENT)

K TO ADVISE.

LVED LINEN

fabrics & trim samples;

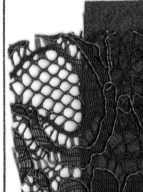

Fashion week
UK
British Fashion Council
www.londonfashionweek.co.uk

USA
Council of Fashion Designers
of America
www.cfda.com

New York Fashion Week
www.mbfashionweek.com

Europe
Milan
www.cameramoda.it

Paris Fashion Week
www.modeaparis.com

Australia
Australian Fashion Week
www.rafw.com.au

Trade shows
Linea Pelle
www.lineapelle-fair.it

Pitti Filati
www.pittimmagine.com

Première Vision
www.premiervision.fr

Rendez-Vous Paris
www.rendez-vous-paris.com

Tissu Premier
www.tissu-premier.com

Trend forecasting

www.carlininternational.com

www.fashioninformation.com

www.kjaer-global.com

www.promostyl.com

www.stylesignal.com

www.thefuturelaboratory.com

www.trendstop.com

Acknowledgements and picture credits

Thanks are due to everyone who helped put this book together: the many designers, creatives and students at Kingston University and London College of Fashion, who showed great generosity in allowing us to reproduce their work. Thank you to all those who agreed to be interviewed: Giles Deacon, Shelley Fox, Richard Nicoll, Markus Lupfer, William Tempest, Colin McNair, Louis Armadola, James New, Kenneth Mackenzie, Sophie Hulme, Will Broome, Ian Garlant, Jens Laugesen, Ohne Titel, Emily Craig, James Spreckley, Simon Kneen, Gordon Richardson, Mark Eley, Sibling, Katie Greenyer, Holly Berry, Bill Amberg and Nicholas Kirkwood. Thanks also go to Katherine Baird at London College of Fashion Archive and to Sifer Design.

Picture credits

Cover image courtesy of Giles Deacon; p 3 courtesy of Poppy Dover; pp 14–15 courtesy of Richard Nicoll; p 17 illustration courtesy of Stephen Jones; p 20 courtesy of Ringhart; pp 22–23 courtesy of Studio M; p 24 courtesy of Holly Berry; p 26 courtesy of Getty Images; p 33 courtesy of Shelley Fox; p 35 courtesy of Danielle Scutt; pp 38-39 courtesy of Giles Deacon; pp 40–41 courtesy of Shelley Fox; p 42 courtesy of Richard Nicoll; p 45 courtesy of Markus Lupfer; pp 46–47 William Tempest; pp 48–49 courtesy of Colin McNair; p 51 courtesy of Brooks Brothers; p 54 courtesy of Corbis; p 58 (right) courtesy of Corbis; p 59 courtesy of Sophie Hulme; p 62 (left) © Australian Wool Innovation owner of The Woolmark Company, courtesy of London College of Fashion; p 66 © PA Photos; p 68 (right) courtesy of Corbis; p 69 (left) courtesy of Corbis; p 73 courtesy of Six Eight Seven Six; pp 74–75 courtesy of Sophie Hulme; pp 76–77 courtesy of Will Broome; p 78 © Australian Wool Innovation owner of The Woolmark Company, courtesy of London College of Fashion; p 81 courtesy of London College of Fashion Archive; p 85 courtesy of Getty Images; p 87 © Australian Wool Innovation owner of The Woolmark Company, courtesy of London College of Fashion; p 89 courtesy of The Convenience store; p 93 (right) courtesy of Banana Republic; p 99 courtesy of Hardy Amies; p 101 courtesy of Jens Laugesen; pp102–103 courtesy of Ohne Titel; p 105 courtesy of DKNY; p 106 courtesy of Reiss; p 108 courtesy of Simon Kneen; p 118 courtesy of Nicholas Kirkwood; p 122 courtesy of Giles Deacon; pp 126–127 courtesy of Eley Kishimoto; pp 128–129 courtesy of Sibling; p 130 courtesy of Katie Greenyer; pp 132–133 courtesy of Holly Berry; pp 134–135 courtesy of Bill Amberg; p 137 courtesy of Nicholas Kirkwood; pp 6, 10, 12, 16, 27, 52, 55, 56, 57, 58, 62 (right), 63, 64, 65, 67, 68 (left), 69 (right), 71, 80, 82, 86, 88, 112, 116, 120 and 123 courtesy of Catwalking.com.

BASICS
FASHION DESIGN

Working with ethics

Lynne Elvins
Naomi Goulder

Publisher's note

The subject of ethics is not new, yet its consideration within the applied visual arts is perhaps not as prevalent as it might be. Our aim here is to help a new generation of students, educators and practitioners find a methodology for structuring their thoughts and reflections in this vital area.

AVA Publishing hopes that these **Working with ethics** pages provide a platform for consideration and a flexible method for incorporating ethical concerns in the work of educators, students and professionals. Our approach consists of four parts:

The **introduction** is intended to be an accessible snapshot of the ethical landscape, both in terms of historical development and current dominant themes.

The **framework** positions ethical consideration into four areas and poses questions about the practical implications that might occur. Marking your response to each of these questions on the scale shown will allow your reactions to be further explored by comparison.

The **case study** sets out a real project and then poses some ethical questions for further consideration. This is a focus point for a debate rather than a critical analysis so there are no predetermined right or wrong answers.

A selection of **further reading** for you to consider areas of particular interest in more detail.

Ethical: aware-ness/ reflect-ion/ debate

Working with ethics

Introduction

Ethics is a complex subject that interlaces the idea of responsibilities to society with a wide range of considerations relevant to the character and happiness of the individual. It concerns virtues of compassion, loyalty and strength, but also of confidence, imagination, humour and optimism. As introduced in ancient Greek philosophy, the fundamental ethical question is *what should I do?* How we might pursue a 'good' life not only raises moral concerns about the effects of our actions on others, but also personal concerns about our own integrity.

In modern times the most important and controversial questions in ethics have been the moral ones. With growing populations and improvements in mobility and communications, it is not surprising that considerations about how to structure our lives together on the planet should come to the forefront. For visual artists and communicators it should be no surprise that these considerations will enter into the creative process.

Some ethical considerations are already enshrined in government laws and regulations or in professional codes of conduct. For example, plagiarism and breaches of confidentiality can be punishable offences. Legislation in various nations makes it unlawful to exclude people with disabilities from accessing information or spaces. The trade of ivory as a material has been banned in many countries. In these cases, a clear line has been drawn under what is unacceptable.

But most ethical matters remain open to debate, among experts and lay-people alike, and in the end we have to make our own choices on the basis of our own guiding principles or values. Is it more ethical to work for a charity than for a commercial company? Is it unethical to create something that others find ugly or offensive?

Specific questions such as these may lead to other questions that are more abstract. For example, is it only effects on humans (and what they care about) that are important, or might effects on the natural world require attention too?

Is promoting ethical consequences justified even when it requires ethical sacrifices along the way? Must there be a single unifying theory of ethics (such as the Utilitarian thesis that the right course of action is always the one that leads to the greatest happiness of the greatest number), or might there always be many different ethical values that pull a person in various directions?

As we enter into ethical debate and engage with these dilemmas on a personal and professional level, we may change our views or change our view of others. The real test though is whether, as we reflect on these matters, we change the way we act as well as the way we think. Socrates, the 'father' of philosophy, proposed that people will naturally do 'good' if they know what is right. But this point might only lead us to yet another question: *how do we know what is right?*

You
What are your ethical beliefs?

Central to everything you do will be your attitude to people and issues around you. For some people their ethics are an active part of the decisions they make everyday as a consumer, a voter or a working professional. Others may think about ethics very little and yet this does not automatically make them unethical. Personal beliefs, lifestyle, politics, nationality, religion, gender, class or education can all influence your ethical viewpoint.

Using the scale, where would you place yourself? What do you take into account to make your decision? Compare results with your friends or colleagues.

Your client
What are your terms?

Working relationships are central to whether ethics can be embedded into a project and your conduct on a day-to-day basis is a demonstration of your professional ethics. The decision with the biggest impact is whom you choose to work with in the first place. Cigarette companies or arms traders are often-cited examples when talking about where a line might be drawn, but rarely are real situations so extreme. At what point might you turn down a project on ethical grounds and how much does the reality of having to earn a living effect your ability to choose?

Using the scale, where would you place a project? How does this compare to your personal ethical level?

01 02 03 04 05 06 07 08 09 10

01 02 03 04 05 06 07 08 09 10

Your specifications
What are the impacts of your materials?

In relatively recent times we are learning that many natural materials are in short supply. At the same time we are increasingly aware that some man-made materials can have harmful, long-term effects on people or the planet. How much do you know about the materials that you use? Do you know where they come from, how far they travel and under what conditions they are obtained? When your creation is no longer needed, will it be easy and safe to recycle? Will it disappear without a trace? Are these considerations the responsibility of you or are they out of your hands?

Using the scale, mark how ethical your material choices are.

Your creation
What is the purpose of your work?

Between you, your colleagues and an agreed brief, what will your creation achieve? What purpose will it have in society and will it make a positive contribution? Should your work result in more than commercial success or industry awards? Might your creation help save lives, educate, protect or inspire? Form and function are two established aspects of judging a creation, but there is little consensus on the obligations of visual artists and communicators toward society, or the role they might have in solving social or environmental problems. If you want recognition for being the creator, how responsible are you for what you create and where might that responsibility end?

Using the scale, mark how ethical the purpose of your work is.

01 02 03 04 05 06 07 08 09 10

01 02 03 04 05 06 07 08 09 10

One aspect of fashion design that raises an ethical dilemma is the way that clothes production has changed in terms of the speed of delivery of products and the now international chain of suppliers. 'Fast fashion' gives shoppers the latest styles sometimes just weeks after they first appeared on the catwalk, at prices that mean they can wear an outfit once or twice and then replace it. Due to lower labour costs in poorer countries, the vast majority of Western clothes are made in Asia, Africa, South America or Eastern Europe in potentially hostile and sometimes inhumane working conditions. It can be common for one piece of clothing to be made up of components from five or more countries, often thousands of miles away, before they end up in the high street store. How much responsibility should a fashion designer have in this situation if manufacture is controlled by retailers and demand is driven by consumers? Even if designers wish to minimise the social impact of fashion, what might they most usefully do?

Traditional Hawaiian feather capes (called `Ahu'ula) were made from thousands of tiny bird feathers and were an essential part of aristocratic regalia worn by men. Initially they were red ('Ahu'ula literally means 'red garment') but yellow feathers, being especially rare, became more highly prized and were introduced to the patterning.

The significance of the patterns, as well as their exact age or place of manufacture is largely unknown, despite great interest in their provenance in more recent times. Hawaii was visited in 1778 by English explorer Captain James Cook and feather capes were amongst the objects taken back to Britain.

The basic patterns are thought to reflect gods or ancestral spirits, family connections and an individual's rank or position in society. No two `Ahu'ula are alike (except for late nineteenth-century replicas). Most capes were designed for specific individuals and it is said that no evil thoughts should cross the person's mind when making the capes; instead their focus should be on the future love, long life, good health, honour and success of the wearer that the cape is for.

The base layer for these garments is a fibre net, with the surface made up of bundles of feathers tied to the net in overlapping rows. Red feathers came from the 'i'iwi or the 'apapane. Yellow feathers came from a black bird with yellow tufts under each wing called 'oo'oo, or a mamo with yellow feathers above and below the tail.

Thousands of feathers were used to make a single cape for a high chief (the feather cape of King Kamehameha the Great is said to have been made from the feathers of around 80,000 birds). Only the highest ranking chiefs had the resources to acquire enough feathers for a full length cape, whereas most chiefs wore shorter ones which came to the elbow.

The demand for specific feathers was so great that they acquired commercial value and provided a full time job for professional feather-hunters. These fowlers studied the birds and caught them with nets or with bird-lime smeared on branches. As both the *'i'iwi* and *apapane* were covered with red feathers, the birds were killed and skinned. Other birds were captured at the beginning of the moulting season, when the yellow display feathers were loose and easily removed without damaging the birds.

The royal family of Hawaii eventually abandoned the feather cape as the regalia of rank in favour of military and naval uniforms decorated with braid and gold. Feather capes were given away or sold for other items. The *'oo'oo* and the *mamo* became extinct through the destruction of their forest feeding-grounds and imported bird-diseases. Silver and gold displaced red and yellow feathers as traded currency and the manufacture of feather capes became a largely forgotten art.

Is it more ethical to create clothing for the masses rather than for a few high-ranking individuals?

Is it unethical to kill animals to make garments?

Would you design and make a feather cape?

Fashion is a form of ugliness so intolerable that we have to alter it every six months.

Oscar Wilde

Further reading

AIGA
Design business and ethics
2007, AIGA

Eaton, Marcia Muelder
Aesthetics and the good life
1989, Associated University Press

Ellison, David
Ethics and aesthetics in European modernist literature
2001, Cambridge University Press

Fenner, David EW (Ed.)
Ethics and the arts: an anthology
1995, Garland Reference Library of Social Science

Gini, Al (Ed.)
Case studies in business ethics
2005, Prentice Hall

McDonough, William and Braungart, Michael
'Cradle to Cradle: Remaking the Way We Make Things'
2002

Papanek, Victor
'Design for the Real World: Making to Measure'
1971

United Nations
Global Compact the Ten Principles
www.unglobalcompact.org/AboutTheGC/TheTenPrinciples/index.html